·汉英对照·

中国历代笑话精选(一)

Selected Jokes from Past Chinese Dynasties (I)

柳间亭　李焕武　编译
玮　平　杨秀标　绘图

华语教学出版社
北　京
SINOLINGUA BEIJING

First Edition 1991
Second Printing 1993
Third Printing 1996

ISBN 7-80052-193-1

Published by Sinolingua
24 Baiwanzhuang Road, Beijing 100037, China
Printed by Beijing Foreign Languages Printing House
Distributed by China International
Book Trading Corporation
35 Chegongzhuang Xilu, P.O. Box 399
Beijing 100044, China

Printed in the People's Republic of China

出版者的话

生活离不开笑话，笑话也离不开生活。

数千年来，勤劳智慧的中国人民在创造了灿烂的古代文明的同时，给后人留下了又一笔丰厚的文化遗产——数以万计的历代笑话。它们或幽默，或讽刺，或诙谐，或辛辣；它们针砭流弊，讥讽陋习，启迪借鉴，弃恶扬善。它们植根于广阔的社会生活，因此枝叶繁茂，历久不衰。

今天我们从这些笑话中精选了数百篇，对文字内容进行了疏通修改，略加注释，配以插图，并附有英译文，辑为若干册，每册百篇左右，奉献给喜爱并希望了解中国历代笑话的中外读者，愿朋友们在笑声中多有收获。

Publisher's Note

Take jokes away from life and you take a good part of life away from man.

Throughout China's history the industrious and ingenious Chinese people, while creating a brilliant ancient civilization, have left succeeding generations a rich cultural heritage of tens of thousands of jokes, spanning many different dynasties. The jokes are humorous, sarcastic, witty, pointed. They unmask corrupt and evil practices, ridicule the ugly and ignorant, and are generally relieving as well as enlightening. Rooted in society at large, they flourish and will always be with us.

We have selected several hundred well-known jokes and added footnotes, illustrations and English translations. Each of the several volumes contains around a hundred jokes. The book is dedicated to international readers fond of China and interested in understanding the country better. We hope these jokes from past Chinese dynasties will offer many amusing insights into the character of the Chinese people.

前　言

笑话是以民间口头创作为主的一种文学形式。它短小精悍，生动活泼，深为人民大众喜闻乐见，历久不衰。

笑话以社会生活为背景，揭露了当时社会上存在的贪婪狡诈，阿谀奉承、迂腐愚昧等各种丑恶现象，也表现了人们的机巧和幽默。不管这些故事如何纷繁多变，但它们总是以笑为生命。往往一件趣事，一个片断，甚至一句警言妙语，通过夸张、想象，而令人情不自禁地捧腹发笑。人们在开心乐怀之余，增长知识，识别生活中的真与假、美与丑、善与恶。

编者从中国历代众多的笑话中，精选了102篇，采取汉英对照，图文并茂的形式，为学习汉语的国外朋友们提供有趣而又有益的读物。这些笑话也反映了中国人民的伦理观，将有助于增进中国人民与各国人民之间的相互了解和友谊。

限于编者水平，书中定有不当之处，盼专家学者和读者们不吝赐教。

编　者

1989.10

Preface

As a humorous form of folk literature among the people, jokes have always enjoyed wide popularity with their short organization and lively language.

Rooted deeply in Chinese societies, these jokes expose all kinds of ugly social phenomena such as greed and deceit, flattery and cruelty, and pedantry and ignorance. Meanwhile, jokes also reflect people's resourcefulness and humour. No matter how colourful or changeable, jokes always enliven with laughter. An intriguing episode or a witty remark can grip the imagination of the listener and through exaggeration can illicit a burst of laughter. In savouring humour, people enrich their knowledge of life and deepen their understanding of the true and the false, beauty and ugliness, and good and evil.

Over 100 jokes from among thousands from different dynasties were carefully chosen and compiled in this book. Illustrated and with English translations, this book should make interesting reading for the student of Chinese. In addition, these jokes offer an insight into the Chinese outlook on morality and ethics, which should prove helpful in the mutual understanding and promotion of friendship between the Chinese people and the people throughout the world.

Due to a limited staff and to time constraints, the compilers would like to apologize for any errors that may surface in the text. All criticism and suggestions on further improvement will be most welcome.

The compilers
October, 1989

目　录

CONTENTS

1. 换靴子

某人有一双厚底靴和一双薄底靴。一天早晨，他错将一只厚底靴和一只薄底靴穿在脚上。他出门去办事，走在路上只觉得一只脚高，一只脚低，非常不舒服。他诧异①地说："真奇怪，今天我的腿怎么变得一长一短了？"

路上有人提醒他说："你是穿错靴子啦。"

他听了这话，急急忙忙回家去换靴子。可是，他到家一看，想了一想说："甭②换啦，家里的也是一厚一薄。"

注 释

① 诧 (chà) 异：惊讶。 Surprisingly

② 甭 (béng)： 方言，用不着，不必。“不 (bú)”，“用 (yòng)” 两字急读的合音。 (Dialect) no need. It is the combination of the two words 不 (bú) and 用 (yòng) when read quickly.

1. Not a Pair Either

A man had two pairs of boots, one with thick soles and the other with thin soles. One morning, he made the mistake of putting one of each of the boots on. While walking, he felt very uncomfortable. “How strange! How is it that my legs aren't the same length today?” He said to himself in surprise.

A passer-by told him, “Your boots aren't a pair.”

Hearing this he hurried home to change boots. But when he got home and saw the other boots, he thought for a moment and said, “There's no need to change. These other two are not a pair either. One is thick and the other thin.”

2. 这个字一夜就长成这么大啦！

有一个读书人教儿子认“一”字，不一会儿，那男孩就记住了。

第二天，那人擦桌子时，随手用抹布在桌面上画了一横，想考一考儿子还认不认识“一”字，那男孩一点也认不出来。

父亲说：“这就是昨天教你的‘一’字呵！”男孩睁大眼睛，吃惊地说：“只隔了一夜，‘一’字就长成这么大啦！”

2. How Big It Has Become Overnight!

One day a scholar taught his son to read the Chinese word "one". Soon the boy learnt it by heart.

The next day while the scholar was wiping the table, he happened to write on the table top a "one" with his wet rag to quiz his son. The boy couldn't read it at all.

"This is the word 'one' I taught you to read yesterday, now isn't it?" said the scholar.

"Oh! But how big it has become overnight!" said the boy in surprise.

3. 黑　豆

从前有一个呆子，运载一车黑豆去集市上卖。过桥的时候，翻了车，黑豆全撒在河里。他急急忙忙回家叫人来捞。

他走后，附近人家乘机把豆全捞走了。那呆子回来时，只见无数蝌蚪在水里游动。他以为这就是黑豆，便同家人准备下水打捞。蝌蚪见了人影，立刻惊散，呆子着急地喊："黑豆呀黑豆，你们不认识我了吗？别逃跑啊！就算你们长了尾巴，我可仍然认得出来啊！"

3. Black Beans

Once upon a time a foolish man carried a cart of black beans to the market to sell. When crossing a bridge, the cart turned over and the beans fell into the river. He went home hurriedly to ask his family to dredge his beans from the river.

After he left, the persons living nearby went into the river and took all the beans away. When the foolish man returned, all he saw in the river were many tadpoles; all of which he mistook for his black beans. He, therefore, got ready to go into the water and collect them with his servants; but the tadpoles, seeing the people enter the river, took flight.

"Black beans, ah, black beans!" the foolish man shouted. "Don't you recognize me? Even though you have grown tails, I can still distinguish your original shape!"

4. 不 公 平

有一个懒汉，什么事情也不想干，只好守在家里喝西北风①。时间一天天地过去了，为了填饱肚子，他不得不打算找个轻活儿干干。

一天，有人向他建议："去看守坟地吧！再也没有比这更轻松的活儿了。"

那懒汉高高兴兴地上工了，但不多久他就撂挑子②了。他逢人便发牢骚："太不公平了！他们全都躺在地上，偏偏让我一个人站着！"

注 释

① 喝西北风：指没有东西吃。 Have nothing to eat.

② 撂挑子：撂，口语，放下。撂挑子即甩手不干。(Colloq.) put down, meaning to stand aside and refuse to do the job any longer.

4. Unfair

Once upon a time there was a lazy fellow who didn't want to work, and stayed home only to suffer from cold and hunger. As time went by, he knew he had to find a job, hopefully an easy one, in order to support himself.

One day someone said to him, "Go to the graveyard! Indeed, there is no easier work to be found."

So the fellow happily went to work, but he soon quit, grumbling to everyone he met, "It's too unfair! They're all lying down, while I have to stand there by myself."

5．明年同岁

杂货商新添了一个女儿。一天，朋友来给他的小千金①说媒②，讲明对方只比女孩大一岁。

商人与妻子私下商量这门亲事，他说："女儿刚满周岁③，而那男孩已经两岁了，比女儿大了一倍。等到女儿二十岁出嫁时，他该有四十岁了。我们怎能忍心让闺女④嫁给这么一个老头子呢？"

他的妻子笑了笑说："你真够笨的！现在我们的女儿一岁，明年她不就同那个男孩同岁了吗？"

注 释

① 千金：尊称别人的女儿。 A respectful form of address for another person's daughter.

② "说媒"句：旧中国有幼年订亲的习俗，称"娃娃亲"。 In ancient China, there was a custom to settle a marriage when one was still very young, called "a baby marriage".

③ 周岁：一岁。 One year old.

④ 闺女：女儿。 Daughter.

5. The Same Age Next Year

A grocer once had a daughter born to him. One day a friend of his made a match for his baby-girl, and told him the future husband was only one year older than she was.

The grocer discussed this marriage in private with his wife. "Our daughter is just one, the boy's age is the double of hers; when she is twenty and gets married, her husband will be forty," he said. "How do we have the heart to marry off our daughter to such an old husband?"

His wife smiled and said, "You're really dumb. Our daughter is now one year old, in one years time she'll be the same age as the boy, now won't she?"

6．靠谁养活

一个五十岁的老人有一个三十岁的儿子。这个儿子非常懒惰，从不干事，衣食全靠父亲供给。

那老人为儿子的事忧心忡忡，便带着儿子一同去算命①。父子俩都相信了算命先生的话：父亲可以活到八十岁，儿子也有六十二岁的寿命。

儿子知道了父亲和自己的寿数②后，非常犯愁③。父亲便安慰儿子说：

"别难过！你才三十岁，还有三十二年的好日子过呢！"

儿子回答说："我并不是担心自己的寿命，而是你的寿命叫我难过。"

父亲听了这话，很受感动，含着泪说："你也不必过于伤心！我还有三十年的寿命嘛！"

儿子说："我倒不是关心你的寿命。我仔细盘算了一下，你要比我早死两年，还有两年我靠谁养活？"

注 释

① 算命：推算人的命运祸福的一种迷信活动。 Fortune telling.

② 寿数：迷信的人认为命中注定的岁数。 Life expectancy as predicted by a fortune teller.

③ 犯愁：方言，发愁。 (Dialect) worry.

6. Whom to Depend on

There once was an old man aged 50, who had a lazy son aged 30. The son couldn't earn his own living, and still depended on his old father for food and clothing.

The old man was very worried about him, so he took him to the fortune teller to have his fortune told. The father and son both believed the fortune teller's prediction that the father would live to 80 and the son to 62.

After having found out how long they were going to live the son was very sad. His father comforted him.

"Don't be so sad! You are only 30 now, and still have 32 years of good days ahead of you."

"I'm not worrying about my own age. It's just your age which causes me great anxiety," the son said.

Upon hearing his words, the father was deeply moved, and in tears said, "Don't worry about me so much! I've got 30 years ahead of me too."

"I'm not worried about your age either," said the son, "I have figured out that you'll die two years earlier than I. So whom will I depend on in the two years after your death?"

7. 死去活来

有一次，一伙当家的①凑在一起议论不怕老婆的问题。他们推选了一人当主席，他是这伙人之中最怕老婆的。会议刚开始，有人慌里慌张地来报告：

"事情很不妙啊！你们的婆娘②探听到你们的活动，已商议好要来围攻了。"

听到这消息，众人惊恐万分，各自夺路而逃。唯独主席却纹丝不动。人们原以为主席这次倒真不怕老婆了，其实呢，他早吓得没魂了。

奇怪的是过了一阵，主席又苏醒了，人们纷纷问他，怎样死去又能活过来，他说："我原是死了的，只是在阴间③碰见前妻，吓得我又赶忙活了回来。"

注释

① 当家的：方言，丈夫。 (Dialect) husband.

② 婆娘：方言，妻子。 (Dialect) wife.

③ 阴间：迷信传说死人所在的地方，也叫阴曹、阴司。 The place where the dead dwell according to superstition. It can also be called 阴曹，阴司。

7. Revival

A group of husbands once put their heads together to discuss how to stand up to their wives. They elected as chairperson the one man among them who most feared his wife. When the meeting began, another person came running in a

flurry, and reported, "You're all in trouble! Your wives have found out about your activities and have agreed to surround and attack you."

The husbands were greatly surprised and frightened at the news, and they scattered in every direction, all, except the chairman, who sat still in his chair without moving. At first the others thought that this time the chairman was really going to stand up to his wife; but in fact, what happened was that he was literally scared to death.

Strangely enough though, after some time passed the chairman regained consciousness. The others, in a state of confusion, asked him how it was that being dead he could come back to life.

He replied, "At first I was dead, but I happened to bump into my wife in the nether world and she scared the living daylights back into me."

8. 莫管它漏水

有一次，一条渡船过河时，船身突然撞上了礁石。河水不断地涌进舱里，旅客们惊慌失措。唯有一位先生没事似地坐着不动，并且讥笑众人大惊小怪。

“用不着急嘛！关咱们什么事，”那人说，“莫①管它漏水！船又不是咱们的。”

注 释

① 莫：不要。 don't

8. It Doesn't Matter If It Is Leaking!

A ferry boat was once crossing a river. Suddenly the boat struck a rock and water relentlessly poured into the cabin. The passengers were frightened out of their wits. Only one man sat calmly as if nothing had happened and even laughed at the way the others were so alarmed.

"Don't worry! It's not our problem," the man said. "It doesn't matter if it's leaking because it's not our boat."

9. 糊涂虫

有一个县官老爷，判案时总是分不清是非、善恶，因此百姓给他取了个“糊涂虫”的诨号，并编了一首诗来嘲讽他：

黑漆皮灯笼，
晴天萤火虫；
粉墙画白虎，
青纸描乌龙；
茄子敲泥磬①，
冬瓜撞木钟；
天昏与地暗，
那管是非公。

这首诗被许多人传抄，并贴满大街小巷。那位糊涂县官也看见了这首诗，立即把手下人叫来训斥一顿：“外面贴出告示，要捉拿糊涂虫，你为什么不抓？我限你三天之内至少抓到三个，缺了一个，决不轻饶。”

那个衙役只得走出衙门，边走边嘀咕：“他妈的！叫我到哪儿去抓糊涂虫？”

刚到城门，他忽然看见一个人头上顶着包袱，骑在马上，觉得很奇怪，于是前去问道：“你为什么不把包袱放在马背上？”

那人答道："我怕马负担太重。我用头顶着包袱，不就可以省点马力吗？"

衙役一听此言说："这家伙可算是一个糊涂虫，带去见官。"

衙役又信步出城，正碰见一个手持长竹竿的乡巴佬②要进城门。他先是竖着竹竿走，城门太低，进不去；然后他横着竹竿进，城门又太窄，仍然过不去。那个乡巴佬在城外徘徊半天，竟不知道怎样才进得城内。

那衙役见此情景，又说："这浑小子③也够得上是个糊涂虫，带他去见官。”还差一个糊涂虫没着落，他只好先把这两个押去。

县官听完两人的傻事后，笑着对骑马的糊涂虫说：“你真够笨的！你头上顶着包袱骑马，岂不是便宜了你那牲口④?!”

他又转向拿竹竿的糊涂虫讥笑地说：“你为什么不把竹竿锯作两段？一条长竹竿成了两段短的，岂不早就进城了？”

衙役一听糊涂官说的糊涂话，连忙跪下禀道：“第三个糊涂虫已经有了。”

县官急忙问：“是谁？还不赶快抓来？”

衙役回答道：“等下一任县官老爷来了，我立刻去捉拿他。”

注 释

① 磬 (qìng)：古代打击乐器，形状象曲尺，多用玉或石制成。 An ancient percussion instrument shaped like a ruler. It is mostly made of jade or stone.

② 乡巴佬：口语，乡下人（含蔑视意）。 (Colloq.) country bumpkin (derogatory).

③ 浑小子：口语，不明事理的人（含贬义）。 (Colloq.) unreasonable man (derogatory).

④ 牲口：家畜，如牛、马、骡、驴。多用于口语。 Domestic aminal, such as cow, horse, donkey, mule, etc., often used in spoken language.

9. An Out-and-out Bungler

Once upon a time there was a leading county official, who when settling lawsuits could never clearly distinguish between right and wrong, truth and falsehood, and merits and demerits. Therefore the people nicknamed him "the bungler", and verses were made up to taunt him:

A lantern covered by a black hide,
Glowworms in the clear sky,
A white tiger drawn on the white wall,
On the dark paper there's traced a black
 dragon,
Wax gourds strike the wooden bell,
The eggplant beats the mud chimes,
A murky sky over the dark earth,
The same between right and wrong.

Soon many people copied these verses and pasted them up on the walls in all the streets and lanes. The bungling official saw these posters and scolded his subordinates.

"Outside there are official notices everywhere, saying there are many bunglers throughout the county. Why aren't you out there arresting them?" He said to one of his messengers. "I will give you three days to arrest at least three bunglers. If you are one short, I will have no mercy!"

The messenger left the government office and on the way loathed, "Damn him! Where am I going to arrest these bunglers?"

At the city gate the messenger happened to see a man riding with a parcel on his head. He went straight up to the man and asked, "Why don't you put the parcel on the horse's back?"

"I'm afraid it will be too heavy for the horse," said the man. "I put the parcel on my head to lighten its burden."

"This fellow can be counted as a bungler," said the messenger upon hearing this. "I'll bring him to the official."

The messenger went back to the city gate again where he fortunately happened to see a country bumpkin holding a long bamboo pole and attempting to go through the city gate. He first tried to enter holding the pole vertically, but the gate was too low. Then, holding it horizontally, he found that the gate was too narrow. Pacing up and down the country bumpkin hadn't the slightest idea of how to get into the city.

"This guy can be counted as a bungler, too. I'll bring him to the official as well," said the messenger upon witnessing this. The messenger took the two men into official custody, and only one bungler was left to be caught.

Having heard the two men's stories, the official laughed at the first bungler and said, "How foolish you are! Carrying the parcel on your head. Isn't this letting your horse take advantage of you?"

"You fool!" the official, turning to the bungler with the pole, sneered, "Why didn't you saw the long pole in two? If the pole had become two short ones, you would have entered the gate!"

Hearing the bungling official's muddled talk the messenger knelt down and reported, "I've found the third bungler."

"Who? Go fetch him quickly," said the official.

"When the next county official arrives, I'll fetch him at once," answered the messenger.

10. 我叫你的儿子也挨冻!

宋朝(960—1279)时，有一个太尉① 很溺爱儿女。一天他回到家中，看见儿子没穿褂子②跪在雪地上。他问明原委，知道是自己的母亲体罚有严重过失的孙子。于是他也光了脊梁③，让人把自己绑上，跪在儿子旁边。

他母亲听说此事，前来问他为什么这样作贱④自己？太尉回答说：

"你冻我的儿子，我也冻你的儿子！"

注 释

① 太尉：宋代武官首脑。 Head military officer in

the Song Dynasty (960-1279).

② 褂子：中式的单上衣。 Chinese-style coat.

③ 脊梁：方言，脊背。 (Dialect) back.

④ 作贱：轻视、侮辱。 Look down upon and insult.

10. I'll Make Your Son Suffer and Catch Cold, Too!

In the Song Dynasty there was a Grand Commander who spoiled his children. One day he came home and saw his son kneeling on the snow covered ground without a coat on. Having asked his son the reasons for such behavior, he discovered that his own mother was punishing her grandson for a wrong-doing. He then took off his own coat, and ordering the servants to tie him up, knelt down on the snow covered ground beside his son.

His mother hearing about this went to ask him what the matter was.

"You're making my son suffer and catch cold. So now I'll make your son suffer and catch cold, too!" said the Grand Commander.

11. 借　牛

某人想向一个财主借牛，于是派仆人给财主送去一封借牛的信。财主正陪着客人，怕客人知道自己不识字，便装模作样地看信。他一边看，一边不住地点头，然后抬头对来人说：“知道了，过一会我自己去好了。”

11. Borrowing a Cow

A man once wanted to borrow a cow from a wealthy man, so he had his servant send a note to the wealthy man. The rich man, who was entertaining some guests, took the note and ashamed to be taken as an illiterate, pretended to be able to read it. When reading it he nodded his head repeatedly.

"I know," the rich man said to the messenger, "I'll go myself in a moment."

12. 死不瞑目

从前有一个贪婪成性的地主快要断气了，躺在床上断断续续地咕哝①。家里的人急着想知道他临终前还有什么话要交待。

儿子低声地问："爸，您老人家还有什么事要嘱咐我们的？"

地主无力地说："那块肉——，我——死不瞑目啊！"

儿子不解地问："什么，哪块肉？"

地主说："那次——我同你几个舅——一块吃饭，可惜——没吃到——那块肉。"

"爸，您为啥不先下筷子？"

"儿呀，筷子上已有一块肉了。"

"那您为啥不赶紧送进嘴里？"

"嘴里——也有一块肉。"

"那您就该快吞下去啊！"

地主叹了一口气说："喉咙里也有——一块肉，我——怎样吞得下去啊！"

注 释

① 咕哝：多指自言自语，带有不满情绪。 Murmur to oneself, often with dissatisfaction.

12. Refusing to Die an Unhappy Death

Once upon a time there was a very greedy landlord who was about to die. He lay in bed, murmuring incomprehensibly. The family members were eager to understand his final words.

"Father, do you have anything else to tell us?" said his son whispering in the father's ear.

"That piece of meat..., I...don't want to...die an unhappy death!" the landlord said weakly.

"What, what meat?" his son asked.

"That time...I had dinner together...

with your uncles. It's a pity . . . I couldn't eat . . . that piece of meat . . . at table," he answered.

"Father, why didn't you try to first move your chopsticks?"

"My son, . . . there was already one piece . . . between the chopsticks."

"Then why didn't you quickly put it in your mouth?"

"In my mouth . . . there already was . . . a piece of meat."

"I say, you should have swallowed it in one gulp!"

"In my throat . . . there was a piece of meat, there too. How could . . . I swallow it?" the landlord sighed.

13. 吃 饼

有一个人饿极了，便到一家小吃店买饼吃。他吃完一个饼不饱，接着吃第二个饼。这样一连吃了六个饼，他还不饱。直到吃完第七个饼，他才感到满足了。可是，这时他突然懊悔起来："唉，早知道这样，我一开始就吃第七个饼，岂不够了，何必白白吃那六个呢!?"

13. Having Cakes

A man was very hungry, and went to buy cakes at a snack bar. When he finished a cake, he found he hadn't had enough, and so ate a second one. He felt so hungry that after eating six cakes in succession, he still hadn't satisfied his hunger. Not till the seventh cake was eaten up, did he feel satisfied. Then, suddenly, he had a feeling of regret.

"Ah, if I had known this before, I would have eaten the seventh cake first and that would have been enough and there would not have been any need to eat those six others."

14. 迷信风水①

一个非常迷信风水的人，凡事都得请教风水先生，预卜凶吉祸福。

一日，他坐在一堵墙下，墙忽然倒塌，把他压在下面。他大喊救命，仆人们走来一看，说："东家，请忍耐一下！我们得先去问问风水先生，看看今天宜不宜动土。"

注 释

① 风水：旧指住宅、坟地等的地理形势。迷信的人认为它影响家族盛衰。风水先生是指靠为他人看风水为生的人。Geomancy, an ancient Chinese superstition concerning the geographic situation of a house or tomb and its relation to the destiny of the family. 风水先生 refers to those who earned their living by advising people on such things.

14. Blind Faith in Geomantic Omens

There once was a man who had a superstitious faith in geomantic omens. He consulted the geomancer beforehand concerning all signs beneficial or unfortunate.

One day, while he was sitting at the foot of a wall, the wall collapsed on top of him. He cried, "Help!" His servants came over to have a look and said, "Be patient, Master. Let's ask the geomancer if it is a good omen to break the ground today."

15. 再喝一碗

一个老奶奶很讲究忌讳①，逢年过节她总是吉利话不离口，从没说过一个“不”字。

一次大年初一②，老奶奶一起床，小孙女就送来一碗甜黏粥，她高兴地喝了。

孙女问：“奶奶，再喝一碗好吗？”

老奶奶回答：“好，好。”

小孙女立刻送来第二碗黏粥，她又喝了。

小孙女问：“再来一碗？”

老奶奶想到年节不能说“不”字，于是说：“好吧，我能喝三碗。”就这样老奶奶一气喝了六碗，她的肚皮被撑得象一面大鼓。

不懂事的小孙女仍一个劲地问：“奶奶，你可愿意再喝一碗？”

老奶奶不由自主地连忙摇手说：“不，不喝了，再喝一点儿，奶奶就要胀死了啊！”

注 释

① 忌讳：由于风俗、习惯的顾忌，使言谈、行为有所隐避，日久成为禁戒。 Taboo, that comes from a custom or habit of talking indirectly about something for fear of ill-luck.

② 大年初一：中国的阴历正月第一天，即传统的春节。The first day of the first lunar month in the Chinese lunar calendar.

15. Some More

Once there was an old grandmother who believed in taboo. On New Year's Day and other festival days, she would try only to say nice things, and never let the word "no" rashly fall from her mouth.

One lunar New Year's Day, as soon as the grandmother got up, her little granddaughter passed her a bowl of sweet rice porridge. She drank it up joyfully.

"Grandma, will you take another bowl of rice porridge?" asked the granddaughter.

"All right," replied the grandmother.

The little girl passed her the second bowl of rice porridge and quickly she drank it.

"Some more rice porridge?" asked the granddaughter.

The grandmother thought that during New Year's Day she couldn't say "no", and so she replied promptly, "O.K., I'll drink a third bowl." In this way the grandmother drank six bowls, and her stomach was like a big drum.

The little girl who wasn't very sensible still asked persistently, "Grandma, would you like to drink some more sweet rice porridge?"

The grandmother couldn't help shaking her hand, and said hurriedly, "No, no, no more, no more! If I drink any more, I'll bloat myself to death."

16. 酒　徒

有嗜酒者，在一次宴席上醉得站不起来。主人婉劝他回家，说：“天快要下雨啦！”

醉汉说：“下雨了，叫我如何回去？”

一会儿，主人又说：“雨已经不下了。”

“既然雨停了，何必叫我早回去！”说完，又继续痛饮不已。

16. A Taste for Wine

A man had a taste for wine. One day at a dinner party, he drank so much he couldn't leave his seat. The host urged him to go home quickly, and said, "It's going to rain."

"If it rains, how shall I go home?" he said.

After a while, the host said again, "The rain has stopped."

"Since the rain stopped, there's no need to go home so early," he said, continuing to drink his fill.

17 买红蜡烛的钱为什么记在我帐上？

从前，有一个县丞不识字，买东西都用图代替文字记帐。

一天，县丞外出时，知县来到衙门，偶然看到那本奇怪的帐簿。他对帐簿上的图画迷惑不解，便用朱笔把所有的图都划掉了。

县丞返回衙门后，发现帐簿中有许多红杠杠，勃然大怒说："你儿子买的红蜡烛，为什么也记在我的帐上？"

17. Why Did You Charge the Red Candles to My Account?

The story goes that a magistrate's assistant hadn't learned to read, and all purchases were charged to his account with pictures instead of words.

One day when the assistant was out, the magistrate went into his government office and happened to read this strange account book. He was puzzled by the pictures in the book and proceeded to cross out all the pictures with a writing brush dipped in red ink.

When the assistant returned, and found all those red lines in his account book, he flew into a rage and said, "Your son bought these red candles, why have they been charged to my account?"

18. 吝啬鬼

过去有一个从不请客的吝啬鬼。一天邻居借用他的房子宴请宾客，有人来问吝啬鬼的仆人："你的主人果真要请客吃饭吗？"

那仆人说："你想要我家主人请客，那就等到下辈子吧！"

几天后，吝啬鬼知道了仆人讲过的这句话，就不依不饶地骂道："谁准许你答应那家伙下辈子来我家吃饭！？"

18. A Miser

There was a miser who never entertained any guests. One day his next-door neighbour used his place to hold a party, some people hearing of this asked the miser's servant, "Is it true that your master is really going to entertain guests?"

"If you think my master is going to entertain guests, well, you'll just have to wait until the next life."

A few days later the miser after hearing about what the servant had said, poured out a stream of abuse, "Who allowed you to ask that fellow to have dinner in my home in the next life?"

19. 道学①先生

道学先生迈着八字步在大街上行走时，天下起了大雨，他也跟众人急匆匆地跑起来。

跑了一阵子，他猛然省悟到举止有失检点。便懊悔地说："跑有失尊严，君子有过则改！"

于是他冒着雨退回起跑处，然后斯斯文文②地、慢慢地向前走去。

注 释

① 道学：这里指古板迂腐的意思。 Here it means "obstinate and off-date".

② 斯斯文文：斯文的强调形式，文雅的。 The stressed form of 斯文, meaning refined.

19. The Confucian Moralist

Once upon a time there was a Confucian moralist who, when in the street, walked with carefully measured steps. One day it suddenly began raining cats and dogs and following the crowd, he ran along hastily.

After running for a while, the moralist came to realize that he was careless about his manner and said, "Running is undignified. A gentleman corrects mistakes regretfully if he has made any."

So he returned in the rain to the place where he had begun running, and then walked along gently and slowly.

20．谁知道你们俩可以卖的？

一位店老板有一个儿子。一天，他要出门办货，临走时嘱咐儿子照看好生意。

一会儿，一位远客进店问："有大人在家吗？"

男孩回答："没有。"

"那你的父母呢？"

"也没有。"

店老板回家后，了解到这桩事，就批评儿子说："你为什么对客人说没有父亲和母亲？"

儿子理直气壮地回答：“谁知道你们俩可以卖的？”

20. Who Knew You Two Could Be Sold?

A shopkeeper had a little son. One day he was going out to purchase goods, and before leaving he told his son to look after the business.

Soon a guest from afar came into the shop, and asked, "Are there any grown-ups home?"

"No," the boy answered.

"And your parents?"

"No, don't have any either."

The shopkeeper came home and having learned of this, he criticised his son, and said, "Why did you answer that you have no father and mother?"

"Who knew you two could be sold?" the boy replied reasonably.

21. 死错了人

有一个财东死了丈母娘，准备去祭奠，请了一位私塾①先生写一篇祭文。那位先生不肯动脑子写文章，照书本抄了一篇祭丈人的文章交差。

有人看出毛病，对财东讲了。那位私塾先生自然受到一番责怪。但他很不服气地说："书上写得明明白白，如何有错？只怕是你家死错了人，怎能怪我？"

注 释

① 私塾：旧时家庭、家族设立的学堂。 The private school in the old days.

21. Mistaking the Dead

Long ago a rich man's mother-in-law died, and he wanted to hold a memorial ceremony for her, so he asked a teacher in a private school to write a funeral essay. The teacher, unwilling to write it himself, copied an essay to a father-in-law from a classical book.

The rich man was told about this mistake and he promptly blamed the teacher for it. But the teacher was not taken aback.

"It's written very clearly in the classical book," he said, "If there is a mistake, perhaps it is the dead who has been mistaken, so don't blame me for that!"

22. 决不赊帐

从前，一个吝啬的人发了财。后来，他得了重病，眼看就要断气了。他有气无力地恳求妻子说：“我一生爱惜钱财，断了所有的亲戚来往，才发了家。我死后，你要剥我的皮卖给皮匠；割我的肉卖给肉铺子；剔出我的骨头熬油，卖给油贩子。”

没等到妻子的应承，他便死了。过了一会儿，他又活转过来，说出了最后的交待：“眼下世人不讲信用，对他们决不能赊帐！”

22. Don't Sell Them on Credit

Long ago a stingy man, after having gotten rich, became seriously ill and was breathing his last breaths. Begging his wife, he said weakly, "I've been in love with money all my life, I broke with all the relatives, and today I'm rich. When I die, you'll take my skin off and sell it to the cobbler; cut away my flesh and sell it to the butcher's shop; make oil with my bones and sell it to the oil vendor.

He died before his wife could answer him. But after a while he came back to life again and said his final words, "Nowadays people don't keep their word. Be sure not to sell them on credit!"

23. 鼻子是他自己咬掉的

甲乙两人打架，甲猛地一口把乙的鼻子咬下来。乙忍着疼痛，揪甲到县官那里告状。

县官问甲："你怎么敢咬掉乙的鼻子？"

甲回答："鼻子是他自己咬掉的，与我无关。"

县官大声斥责道："胡说！人的鼻子比嘴高，自己的嘴怎么能够得着自己的鼻子？"

甲诡辩说："他是站到凳子上够着了的。"

县官恍然大悟，微微点头说：“啊，原来是这么一回事！”

23. He Bit off His Own Nose

Two men, A and B, once came to blows, A bit off B's nose, so B, in much pain, took A to the county magistrate to have the case judged.

"How dare you bite off B's nose!" the magistrate said.

"B bit off his own nose, this has nothing to do with me." A answered.

"Nonsense! Everybody knows the nose is higher than the mouth. How can the mouth reach the nose?" the official said severely.

"By standing on a bench," A said cunningly.

"Oh, so that is how it is!" said the official nodding his head slightly.

24. 藏 肉

一个厨子在自己家里切肉，他习惯地偷偷将一块肉藏到衣襟里。他的婆娘看见了，骂道："肉是自己家的，藏什么？真丢人现眼！"

厨子尴尬地说："我忘了是在自己家做活儿。"

24. Hiding Meat

There was once a cook chopping meat up at home. Through habit he secretly took a piece of meat and hid it in his jacket front. His wife glanced at him and cursed, "This meat is ours, why are you hiding it? Really shame on you!"

"I forgot I'm home," the cook said embarrassingly.

25. 父亲烧掉了

从前，有一个人要出门四、五天，他对儿子交待："有人问我在不在家，你要回答他出门办事去了。一定要把话讲清楚些！"

那人考虑儿子有点傻呵呵①的，就将嘱咐写在纸上，便离家走了。男孩怕忘记了父亲的话，经常念那张纸条。三天过去了，没有客人来访，那个头脑简单的男孩以为纸条没用处了，便把它烧掉了。

第四天头上，他父亲的一位好朋友来了，问道："你爸在家吗？"

那孩子找不到条子，只得说："不在了。烧掉了！"

来客听到噩耗②，非常吃惊，又问："什么时候火化的？"

男孩毫不含糊地回答："昨儿晚上。"

注 释

① 傻呵呵：糊涂不懂事或老实的样子。 Muddleheaded or simple-minded.

② 噩耗：指亲近或敬爱的人死亡的消息。 The news about the death of a close and beloved person.

25. Father Was Burned

Once upon a time, a man went away from his home for four or five days, and said to his son, "If someone asks you where your father is, tell them that he is out on business. Be sure to speak clearly!"

Thinking that his son was a little foolish, the man wrote his instructions on a piece of paper. After his departure the boy, being afraid of forgetting his father's words, read the note from time to time.

The first three days there were no visitors, therefore the simple-minded boy thought the note was useless and burned it.

On the fourth day a close friend of his father's came.

"Is your father in?" the friend asked.

The boy couldn't find the note anywhere, and could only say, "No, not here, burned."

The friend was astonished at the bad news, and asked again, "When was he burnt?"

"Yesterday evening," the boy answered clearly and distinctly.

26. 不识镜

从前，有一少妇从来没有照过镜子。一天，她男人买了一面镜子给她。照镜时，她大惊失色，急忙跑去向婆婆告状。

她抱怨说：“看你的儿子又领了一个新媳妇来家了！”

婆婆惊讶地问：“真有这回事吗？我去看看。”当老太婆面对着镜子时，她也感到迷惑不解，低声说："这到底是怎么一回事？新媳妇的娘怎么也一块儿来了呢？"

26. Not Knowing of The Mirror

The story goes that there was a young woman who didn't know what a mirror was. One day her husband bought one for her. While looking in the mirror she was surprised and hurriedly ran to tell her mother-in-law.

"Your son has brought a new wife home!" the woman complained.

"Really?" the old woman asked surprisedly. "Let me have a look." As soon as she faced the mirror, the old woman became perplexed and confused too. "Now what's all this about?" she murmured. "The bride's mother has come too!"

27. 半边眉毛

有一个恶少没有钱过年，他的妻子为这事很发愁。那人说："你尽管放心，我能弄到过年的钱。"

一会儿，他看见一个剃头匠①从门前经过，便灵机一动，想出了一条妙计。他叫住剃头匠，给自己理发。

恶少说："把眉毛给我剃掉！"

半边眉毛刚刚剃完，他就大叫起来："哪有连人家的眉毛也剃去的？真是天下奇闻啊！"说完，

便揪住剃头匠的衣领，威胁说要把他交给衙门②惩治。

剃头匠慌了手脚，只得拿出一百个铜钱了事。那恶少讹诈到了钱，过了个好年。

妻子看到他少了半边眉毛，提议说："你最好把那半边眉毛也剃掉算了。"

那恶少说："你懂个啥？你不知道我下一步的打算。留着这半边眉毛，好过正月十五③啊！"

注 释

① 剃头匠：走街串巷的理发师付。 A barber who goes along the street to solicit business.

② 衙门：旧时称各级地方行政机关。 The local administrative office in the old days.

③ 正月十五：中国传统的佳节——元宵节。 The Chinese Lantern Festival on the 15th of the first lunar month.

27. One Eyebrow

A rascal had no money for the New Year's Day and this worried his wife. The rascal said, "you may rest assured, everything will be all right."

Later when he saw a barber passing by, he had a brainstorm, and he thought up a clever scheme. He asked the barber to give him a hair cut.

"Could you cut my eyebrows off," said the rascal after the barber had begun cutting.

When one of his brows was shaved, he shouted, "Barbers never cut eyebrows! This is an unheard of absurdity!" With these words the rascal seized the barber by the collar, and took him to the court to seek justice.

The barber was frightened, and had to pay 100 copper cash to settle the matter. Having extorted the money, the rascal spent a happy New Year's Day.

Seeing that one of her husband's eyebrows had disappeared, his wife suggested, "You'd better have the other brow shaved off too."

"Don't you understand what my next move is?" said the rascal. "This brow will be left for the Lantern Festival."

28. 腹中空空如也①

有一个读书人准备去赶考②，他日夜发愁，那副怪模样弄得妻子莫名其妙。

她说：“瞧你那窝囊样，难道男人写文章比女人生孩子还不好受吗？”

读书人叹道：“女人生孩子比起写文章来，总还是容易些呵！”

女人又问：“为什么？”

读书人回答：“女人肚子里有孩子，总是能生下来的，而我腹中空空如也，怎么能写出文章来呢？”

注 释

① 腹中空空如也：此处指学识浅薄。 Here it means "ignorant".

② 赶考：去参加封建时代的科举考试。 Go to take the imperial examination in the feudal society.

28. Nothing in the Head

A scholar was preparing to take the civil examinations. His wife was very puzzled by his constant worrying.

"Look at you, you worthless wretch," she said. "You probably think that it's more difficult for a man to write an essay than for a woman to give birth to a child."

"It is easy for you women to give birth to children," the scholar sighed.

"How's that?" she asked.

"You women can bear children easily because you carry the child in your stomach," the scholar said. "But I have nothing in my head, so how do you expect me to think of something to write?"

29. 扛他回家来！

从前，有一个人欠下许多债，不得不东躲西藏。有一个债主很生气，打发仆人去找他。仆人临走时，那人再三叮嘱：

“见到他时，千万别让溜了。要是不肯来，你扛也得把他扛回家来！”

仆人好不容易找到了那个负债人，二话不说，扛起他就走。在途中，仆人累得再也挪不动步，想歇歇脚。那人在肩上说：“快走啊！要是你停下来喘口气①，让别的债主看到了，把我扛走，那可别怪我呀！”

注 释

① 喘口气：口语中指短暂的休息。 An informal way of indicating a short break.

29. Shoulder Him Home!

There was once a man who was in debt to many, many people and had no choice but to run and hide. One of the creditors was very angry with him, and ordered a servant to look for the man. When the servant left, the creditor said repeatedly.

"If you find him, don't let him slip away. If he isn't willing to go with you, carry him home on your shoulder."

The servant had no easy time finding the debtor and without saying a word lifted him on his shoulder and headed for home. On the way, the servant became too tired to go any further, and was in need of a rest.

"You had better go quickly!" the man on the servant's shoulder said, "If you stop for a rest, the other creditors will find me and will take me away themselves. If that happens, don't blame me."

30．少了一笔利钱

有一个放印子钱①的人丢失了一包银子，碰巧被人拾着，原封不动地还给了他。那放印子钱的人仔细地清点之后，又呆呆地盯了银子好一会儿，紧紧皱起眉头。

拾着银子的人问："你的银子少了吗？"

他痛心地说："银子倒也没少，只是白白地少了一笔利钱！"

注 释

① 印子钱：高利贷的一种。 A kind of usury.

30. Losing Interest

One day a usurer lost a pack of silver ingots. A man happened to find it, and returned the pack to him untouched. Having checked the silver ingots carefully, the usurer stared at it quite a while, and drew together his brows.

"Are there any silver ingots missing?" asked the man who had picked up the silver.

"The silver ingots are all here, but I needlessly lost a lot of interest," he said regretfully.

31. 休 妻

从前，有一个迂夫子新娶了一房①妻室。她长得既美丽，又有才学。那人非常迷恋自己的女人。

一年后，妻子生下了一个男孩，他非常高兴，便陪同妻子回娘家小住。

一进丈母娘家的门，他便看见一个老太婆站在门前，满脸皱纹，眼斜嘴歪，老态龙钟。那迂夫子见丈母娘这样丑陋不堪，回家后便把妻子休②了。

那女人临行前问道：“我究竟有什么过失？你为什么要休弃我？”

迂夫子说：“前几天见你娘老得那么难看，我担心你将来老了也是这般模样，我如何消受得了？我就是因为这个才休了你。”

注 释

① 房：量词，此处用于妻子。 Measure word, here used with wife.

② 休：男子抛弃妻子叫“休妻”。 Desert one's wife.

31. Forsaking One's Wife

Once upon a time, a pedant married a lady who was very beautiful, talented and learned. He was very infatuated with his wife.

A year later, the woman gave birth to a boy. The man was extremely happy and accompanied his wife to her parent's home to stay for a few days.

As soon as he entered his mother-in-law's house, he saw an old woman standing in front of the door. The old woman had a wrinkled face, crooked mouth, was cross-eyed, and was doddering with age. Seeing his mother-in-law so ugly, the pedant forsook his wife and went home.

"Tell what fault I have? Why did you forsake me?" the woman asked on parting.

"When I saw your mother the other day, she was very ugly with age. I'm afraid that you will be as ugly as she is in your old age. Tell me, how shall I bear that?" the pedant said. "I forsook you simply for that."

32. 知 了

从前，有一个东家待佣人非常刻薄，经常缺衣少食。临近夏末，一个佣人听到知了在树上鸣叫，不由感慨万端。他忍不住对东家说："请问东家，知了靠吃什么而生活？"

东家轻蔑地回答："什么也不吃，只吸露珠。"

佣人又问："知了穿什么呢？"

东家不耐烦地说："不穿什么，它有翅膀。"

佣人愤愤地说："那么，你就雇知了当佣人好啦！"

32. A Cicada

A master once treated his servants very meanly, and never even supplied enough food and clothes for them. By the end of the summer, hearing a cicada chirping in the trees, a servant had all sorts of feelings well up in his mind and couldn't help asking his master.

"Would you kindly tell me what the cicada eats?"

"It doesn't eat anything but the dew," answered the master scornfully.

"Does the cicada wear anything?" asked the servant again.

"No, it only has wings," said the master impatiently.

"Then, it is just right for you to employ it as your servant!" the servant said resentfully.

33. 聪明的舅舅

一个村子里住着一家人，愚蠢极了。一天，他家的牛偷吃罐子里的粮食，牛头卡在罐子里出不来了。全家人不知道怎么办才好，就去请舅舅来解难。

舅舅来了，看了一看，果断地说："这事好办，把牛头砍下来不就成了！"

一个外甥按舅舅的意思，砍下了牛头，但牛头仍卡在罐子里出不来。全家人感到束手无策，又向舅舅请教。

舅舅洋洋自得地说："这还不容易，把罐子敲碎！"

罐子敲破，牛头"刷"地掉下来。全家人齐声赞叹舅舅聪明盖世，而此时舅舅反倒哭了。大家很纳闷，问他为何这般伤心？

舅舅擦着眼泪说："我太老了，终究要归天①的。要是我死了，你们再遇到麻烦事，靠谁来帮助你们呢？"

注 释

① 归天：人死去的委婉说法。 An euphemism for "to die".

33. A "Clever" Uncle

Once upon a time there was a family in a village. The members of the family were all very ignorant. One day while eating grain from a pot, their cow got its head stuck in the pot and couldn't get it out. Not knowing what to do, they invited their uncle to come and solve this difficult problem.

The uncle entered their house and had a look. "That's an easy matter," he said in a decisive manner. "Cut off the cow's head!"

One of the nephews cut off the cow's head according to his uncle's idea, but the head was still stuck in the pot. They felt quite helpless and had to consult the uncle again.

"That's easy, just break up the pot!" the uncle said complacently.

As soon as the pot was broken up, the cow's head came out without a problem. Everybody praised the uncle for his uncomparable cleverness. On the contrary, at this moment the uncle burst out crying. They felt puzzled and asked him why he had become so sad.

The uncle wiped his eyes. "I'm now too old and won't live long, I'll die some day after all. Who'll come to help you out if you have any troubles then!" said the uncle.

34. 六条腿和四条腿

从前，一个差役要送一份紧急公文，上司怕误了日期，拨了一匹快马给他。那差役没骑马，而是牵着马急匆匆往前赶路。

过路人看了，觉得很奇怪，问他："你为什么有马不骑啊？"

那差役自以为是地说："六条腿总比四条腿跑得快，是不是这个理？"

34. Six Feet and Four Feet

Once upon a time a messenger was going to deliver an urgent document. His superior was afraid of delay and set aside a very fast horse for him. The messenger, instead of riding it, hurriedly led the horse down the road.

"Why don't you ride the horse?" said a passer-by who saw this strange apparition.

"Six feet run faster than four feet, don't they?" said the messenger, considering himself right.

35. 相 面

有一次，一个傻子在街上闲逛，遇见了一位算命先生。

算命先生正在街头招揽生意，他有声有色地念道："男人手如绵，身边有闲钱。妇人手如姜，财谷满仓箱。不信请来试试呵！"

傻子听了这番话，又笑又拍掌。他大声说："我老婆的手就同姜一样啊！"

一个人知道傻子的底细，故意说："我不信！"

傻子指着自己的脸颊说："你不信？来看我这儿！昨日老婆打我一个嘴巴，到现在我脸上还又红又辣呢！"

35. Reading Faces

A fool once walked along the streets and met a fortune teller.

The fortune teller was soliciting for business at the street corner. "If a man's palm is as soft as cotton, he is sure to have spare cash," he said dramatically. "If a woman's palm is as rough as ginger she is sure to have a lot of grain in the barn and money in the chest. Please try me for that!"

Hearing this nonsense, the fool clapped and laughed. "My wife's hand is as rough as ginger!"

"I don't believe you," said a man on purpose, who had known his ins and outs.

"Don't you believe me? Come and look here!" the fool said pointing to his own face. "Yesterday my wife slapped me here on the face, even now it is still red and hot."

36. 原来书是印出来的!

一个青年整天游手好闲，不愿读书。他的父亲很生气，把他关在书房里，要他目不斜视，全神贯注地读三天书。

三天过去了。当父亲来查看儿子的念书情况时，那青年人兴奋地说："爸，您老人家的教导真是妙极了。这三天使我懂得了许多事情。"

父亲听了，喜形于色地说："好呀，你谈谈三天读书的体会吧。"

青年人自鸣得意地说："我原先以为书是用毛笔写成的，经过三天仔细地观察，我才明白了书全都是印出来的!"

36. So a Book Is Printed!

A young man once idled about all day long, and was not willing to study. For this reason his father was very angry; and locked him in the study. He told his son to fix his eyes on the book and read it attentively for three days.

Three days later when the father went to examine his son's book learning, the son said cheerfully, "Father, your instruction is wonderful. I've understood a lot in the past three days."

Hearing this, his father was obviously pleased and said, "Well, say something about your learning experience in the last few days then."

"I had always considered a book to be written with a writing brush," said the young man, thinking no end of himself. "But after three days carefully studying this book, I have come to realize that a book is printed!"

37. 割股救亲

一个人的父亲患了重病，请了医生到家看病。医生给病人诊脉后说：“令尊的病很难治了，除非你十分孝顺，割下胳膊上的一块肉入药，才可搭救。”

“这很好办。”那人说完，拿了一把刀子出去了。

碰巧，一个外乡人躺在大门外，他立刻在那人的胳膊上动手割肉。那人疼得嗷嗷直叫。

他宽慰地说：“不要喊叫啊！割股救亲是人人称颂的好品德嘛！”

37. Cut off a Piece of Flesh from the Arm to Cure Parent's Illness

Once upon a time, a man sent for a doctor because his father was seriously ill. Having felt the pulse, the doctor said, "It will be hopeless to cure your father, unless you are very filial, that is, if you cut off a piece of flesh from the arm to put into the medicine."

"This will be easy," said the man, bringing out a knife.

He ran into a stranger lying outside the front door, and then he started to cut the stranger's arm. The stranger cried with pain.

"Don't cry out!" the man said comforting him. "To cut off a piece of flesh from the arm in order to cure your father's illness is recognized by everyone as being of high moral character."

38. 剪箭杆

从前，有一个士兵在一次战斗中腿部中箭，疼痛不已。长官请了一位外科①医生来治他的箭伤。

医生看了看说："这个不难！"便拿出一把剪刀，将露在外边的箭杆剪掉，然后就索取手术费要走。

士兵发急地说："剪掉箭杆子谁不会？我要你拔出射进肉里的箭头呀！"

医生摇摇头说："外科的事我已做完，挖掉肉里的箭头那是内科的事。"

注　释

① 外科：指以手术为主要手段治疗疾病的医科。与此相

对，内科指以药物为主要手段治疗内脏疾病的医科。这里“内”“外”相对，指借的是其字面意义。

Surgical department, referring to the branch of medicine that treats diseases mostly by means of surgery. In contrast, 内科 refers to the treatment of inner-body diseases mostly through medicine. Here 内 and 外 are used literally to mean physical problems beneath or on the surface of the skin.

38. Cutting off the Arrow Shaft

Long, long ago, in a battle a soldier was shot in the leg, and suffered from constant pain. An officer in the troop sent for a surgeon versed in external medicine to treat the soldier's wound.

The surgeon came to have a look, then said, "This is easy!" He cut off the arrow shaft at the leg with a big pair of scissors, and immediately asked for fees for the surgical operation.

"Anyone can do that," the soldier, getting upset, cried, "The arrowhead is still in the leg, why haven't you taken it out?"

"My surgical operation is finished. The arrowhead in your leg should be cured by a physician who practices internal medicine."

39. 称心如意

有两个青年同时向一家闺女求婚。一个青年住村东，长得丑但富有；另一个住村西，长得俊却贫寒。姑娘家的父母想先听听女儿的意见。

姑娘对婚姻大事心乱如麻，思考了好一阵，她终于有了一个好主意。

她羞羞答答地对母亲说："那两个青年人的求婚，我都愿意接受。"

母亲一听，直摇头说："闺女，那可不行。"

姑娘回答："娘，行啊！我想最好在村东家吃饭，在村西家睡觉。这样才称心如意啊！"

39. After My Own Heart

Once there were two young men, who went together to make an offer of marriage to a girl. One of them, who lived in the east of the village, was ugly but rich; the other, who lived on the west side of the same village, was handsome but poor. The girl's parents asked for the opinion of their daughter.

The girl was puzzled about the marriage. Having pondered for some time, the girl came up with a good idea.

"I'll accept both proposals," she said to her mother shamefacedly.

"That won't do, my girl," the mother said.

"Yes it will, mother dear," the girl said, "I can have dinner in the east, and live in the west. That is just what my heart desires!"

40. 一钱[1]如命

一个人异常吝啬。一次在旅途中，他遇到河水暴涨，舍不得出摆渡钱，便拼命淌水过河。不料走到河中间时，被洪水冲倒，漂流了半里多路。

他儿子站在岸上，眼看父亲快要溺死了，便急急忙忙找船去搭救父亲。船夫要一钱银子方肯救人，儿子只出五分，两人讨价还价，争执不休。

眼看那落水人快要淹死了，忽然，他从河水中挣扎出头大喊："儿啊，儿啊！五分便救，一钱不救啊！"终于，他被激流吞没了。

注 释

① 一钱：此处钱是量词，一钱等于十分，十钱等于一两。
Measure word here (1钱 = 10分, 10钱 = 1两).

40. Life Is Worth a Penny

Once there was an extremely miserly man who, during his travels, came to a river that was flooding. Since he wasn't willing to pay the ferryman to make the crossing, he decided to walk across it himself. With great effort he got to the middle of the river when the flooding water washed him more than half a *li* downstream.

His son, standing on the bank, seeing his father drowning, looked for someone to save his life. The ferryman asked for a *qian (5grams)* of silver, the son only agreed to give him five *fen* (half a *qian*); they haggled with each other relentlessly.

The man was nearly drowned, but his head struggled out of the water in desperation. "My son, ah, my son! Let him save my life for five *fen*. Don't agree on a *qian*!" the man yelled to his son.

In the end he drowned in the waves.

41. 爱面子

从前，一个人脑子很迟钝，而他的女人却很机灵，又非常爱面子，常常装阔气。

一天，那人在街上碰到朋友，朋友微笑着向他招呼：

“喂，今天你的脸上红扑扑的，早晨喝酒了吧？”

那人如实回答：“没有啊，早晨只吃了两个玉米饼子。”

回家后，他女人听到此事，便开导说：“你应该回答‘喝了酒’，以显示我们家富有。”

次日，他又碰到了那位朋友，朋友还是问他："今早晨喝了酒吗？"

那人回答："是的，喝了一点酒。"

朋友又问："凉的还是热的？"

那人木讷①地回答："蒸的。"

朋友微笑着说："今天早晨你仍是吃玉米饼子。"

那人回到家中，受到他女人的奚落②："你真傻！为什么说酒是蒸的？你不会说是热的酒吗？"

第三天，他又与那位朋友在街上相逢。他就依着妻子的指点，抢先表白说："今早我喝了热酒。"

朋友诘问他："喝了多少？"

他伸出两个指头说："两个。"

朋友大笑道："哈哈！你还是吃了两个玉米饼子。"

注释

① 木讷：迟钝而不善辞令。 Slow witted and inarticulate.

② 奚落：嘲讽、埋怨。 Scoff at.

41. Saving Face

Long ago there was a man who was rather slow in thinking. His wife was very clever, was much concerned about saving face, and always tried to pretend that she was rich.

One day the man met a friend in the street, and the friend greeted him with a smile.

"Hello! You have a high colour today. Did you have a drink this morning?"

"No, I only had two pieces of steamed corn bread," the man replied frankly.

After he got home, his wife was told about this and she enlightened him. "You ought to answer 'yes', in order to display our riches," she said.

The next day when he met his friend again, they talked as the last day.

"Did you have a drink this morning?" asked the friend.

"Yes, I drank a drop of wine," answered the man.

"A cold or a hot drink?"

"Steamed," he said awkwardly.

"Oh, you had steamed corn bread this morning too," the friend said smiling.

When the man returned home, his wife scoffed, "How foolish of you! Why did you say the wine was 'steamed'? Haven't you learned to say 'hot drink'?" she said.

On the third day as soon as he met that friend, the man tried to be the first to speak and said as his wife instructed him, "I've had a hot drink this morning."

"How much did you have?" the friend asked.

"Two pieces," the man replied, stretching out two fingers.

"Aha!" his friend burst out laughing, "Then you had two pieces of steamed corn bread!"

42. 烂盆子

有一位新官上任时，向神发誓："我要是左手要钱，就烂左手；右手要钱，就烂右手。"不久，有人以重金向他行贿，那官手痒，想收下，又怕违背了誓言，神要罚他。

那官苦思冥想，忽然心生一计，叫人拿来一个盆子，让行贿人将钱放在盆子里，再捧进去。以后照此办理，来者不拒。他的两手不但没烂，而且越发白胖了。

他心里暗喜，自言自语地说："当时幸好发誓烂手，我可从来没有用手去拿钱。即便要烂也该烂那盆子，与我毫不相干。"

42. Let the Pot Rot

Once upon a time a new government official upon taking up his official post, vowed to God, "If my left hand receives unwarranted money, may it rot; and so with my right hand." Soon somebody tried to give him a lot of money as a bribe, the official had an itch to get the money, but he was afraid to go back on his vow and face being punished by God.

The official racked his brains and finally came up with a plan. He had a messenger take an empty pot and ordered the briber to put the money in it and then took the dish. Afterwards in this way he never refused anybody's offer. And while his two hands didn't rot, they got white and fat.

Inwardly he rejoiced to himself. "It's fortunate for me that the vow was for my hands to rot, and since the beginning my hands have never taken any money. So if God wants to rot something, he should rot the pot, and that doesn't concern me at all,"

43. 急性子

一个急性子路过一家小饭铺，他大声嚷：“干吗还不上面条？”

店小二匆忙来到跟前，将一碗面条放到桌上，说：“快吃！”那人刚要吃面条，店小二却一手将碗拿走，说：“先生，对不起，该要洗碗了！”

那人回家后，恼怒地对妻子说：“今天那店小二快把我气死了！”

妻子听后，立即收拾行李，说：“你快死了，我得改嫁去！”

只过一宿，那女人便另嫁了人。新婚之夜刚过，她便被男人休了。

新丈夫狠狠地对她说："你干吗还不给我生个儿子？所以要休了你！"

43. Impatience

An impatient man once passed a snack bar, and said loudly, "Why haven't the noodles been served yet?"

A waiter came up in a hurry, and put a bowl of noodles on the table. "Take it quickly!" the waiter said. When the man began eating the noodles, the waiter took away his bowl and said, "I'm sorry, it's time to clean the bowl, sir."

Returning home, the man said to his wife in a rage, "Today the waiter nearly made me die with anger!"

Hearing her husband out, sh packed her luggage at once, and said, "Hurry up and die, I want to get remarried."

The woman got married overnight. The wedding night had just passed, and her new husband divorced her, spitefully saying, "You haven't given birth to a son yet, so I'm divorcing you."

44. 这儿没锄！

有一次，农夫从地里空手回家，妻子问他："你的锄头呢？"

他大声说："还放在稻田地里。"

妻子说："天呀！莫大声！别人听见了，会把锄头拿去的。"

夫妇俩赶快到地里去找锄头，没找着。那农夫贴近妻子耳边，小声地说："这儿没锄！"

44. No Hoe Here

A farmer once came home from the rice field, carrying nothing, so his wife asked him where the hoe was.

"In the rice field," he yelled out very loudly.

"For chrissake, don't talk so loud! Somebody will hear you and take our hoe away," his wife said.

The couple went to look for their hoe, but they didn't find it anywhere. The farmer nestled up against his wife and whispered, "No hoe here!"

45．那狗准是在讲话！

从前，一个新官刚上任，便令一个里长上交一百条狗。那里长千方百计搞到了九十九条，凑不足一百之数。他只得锯掉一头羊的两只角，以羊充狗。

当他去衙门上交一百条狗时，新官发现了那条奇怪的狗。他问道："那条狗的嘴为什么老在动？"

里长战战兢兢地说："那狗准是在讲话！"

45. The "Dog" Must Be Talking Now!

The story goes that a new official who had just taken up an appointment, wanted a precinct chief to hand in 100 dogs. The precinct chief used every conceivable method to get 99 dogs, but couldn't gather together 100. He had to saw off the two horns of a sheep to make up the last dog.

When he handed over the 100 dogs to the government office, the official found the strange "dog".

"Why is the dog's mouth moving so frequently?" said the official.

"The dog must be talking now," the precinct chief said in fear and trepidation.

46. 开门七件事

有个妇人嗜酒如命，每日三餐必痛饮烂醉方休。她的男人对此很生气。

男人耐心地规劝她说："开门七件事——柴、米、油、盐、酱、醋、茶，其中没有酒。贤惠的女人该懂得这个道理。"

女人却振振有辞地说："开门七件事当然每天都离不了，而酒则必须在头天晚上准备好，以备第二天饮用。酒比七件事还更要紧，你怎能将酒同开门七件事相提并论呢？"

46. Seven Daily Household Essentials

A woman was very fond of wine. She drank until she was smashed at all three meals of the day. This upset her husband very much.

Her husband advised her patiently. "The seven daily needs of the household are fuel, rice, oil, salt, soya sauce, vinegar and tea, but there's no wine among these. A virtuous woman should understand the reason behind this."

"Certainly we can't live a day without the seven daily household essentials, but wine must be prepared the night before in order for it to be ready for the next day," the woman said plausibly. "Thus, wine is much more important than the seven daily household essentials. How can you even talk about them in the same breath?"

47. 从不让步

有家父子两人都非常恃强好胜，不管遇到什么事情，从不让步。一天，有位客人到家里来，父亲就打发儿子进城买肉，款待客人。

那年轻人买了肉回家，走到城门口，迎面碰上一个也是很固执好胜的汉子。因城门狭窄，又各不让路，双方便瞪着眼，面对面地对峙着。

父亲见儿子去了好一阵还没有回来，便进城去找。在城门口，他看见儿子同一个大汉相峙而立，顿时明白了一切。

这老头子快步冲上前去，对儿子说："儿啊，你先送肉回家去，我替你在这里同这家伙对站！"

47. Never Giving Way to Anybody

An old man and his son were very obstinate in disposition. No matter what they did, they never gave way to anybody. One day a friend came to visit, so the son was sent to town to get some meat. The young man bought the meat, and on his way home, at the city gate he met a rough fellow. Since the gate was so narrow, neither of them gave way to the other, and they stood there face to face.

Discovering that the son had been gone for a long time, the old man himself went to town to look for him. Approaching the city gate the old man saw his son standing opposite a big fellow, and he quickly understood what had happened.

The old man rushed at them and said to his son, "My son, take the meat home first, let me stand here face to face with this fellow."

48. 两姻亲

有两姻亲：一个性子慢，另一个性子急。

两人有一天在街上相遇，各自作揖施礼问好。

慢性子的人说："首先，我很感谢你今年正月送的食品；二月你又亲自前来祝贺内子①的生日……"他一直说到十一月才抬头，但姻亲早已走了。

他不解地自语："我那姻亲为什么火急火燎地就走开了？"

一个路人告诉他："你刚说到一月，你那亲戚就走开多时了。"

注 释

① 内子：对人称自己的妻子。 A term for "wife" used only by the husband when speaking about her with others.

48. Two Relatives Through Marriage

There once were two people related through marriage: one was patient, and the other was impatient. One day they met in the street by chance, and bowed down to each other in greeting.

The man who was patient said, "First I'd like to thank you for the food you gave me in January, and in February you yourself came to celebrate my wife's birthday, . . ."

He continued in this manner and it was only when he came to "November", that he lifted his head and saw that his relative had gone.

"Why did my relative sneak away in such haste?" he wondered to himself.

A passer-by said, "Your relative was long gone when you were talking about January."

49. 全身挂着铜钱①的水牛

一个巡检②上任不久，就下令猎户限期交一只麒麟③。猎人们无法捉到这种神兽，便将一条满身挂上铜钱的水牛充数。当猎人们上交那只假麒麟时，心里七上八下。那巡检见了，反倒高兴地说："要是全身没有铜钱，这只怪兽倒真象一条水牛。"

注 释

① 铜钱：中国古代铜质辅币，圆形，中有方孔。
Chinese ancient currency made of copper, round in shape with a square hole in the middle.

② 巡检：中国宋朝以后设在关隘要地的武官。

Military officer stationed at some pass or strategic point during the Song Dynasty.

③ 麒麟：传说中的一种怪兽，形状象鹿，头上有角，全身有鳞甲。古人认为它象征祥瑞。An ancient legendary animal resembling a deer with horns on its head and scales all over its body.

49. An Ox with Copper Coins All over Its Body

Long ago, there was a military officer who, having been at his post for only a short time, ordered local hunters to bring him a unicorn within a certain time period. The hunters had no way of catching such a supernatural animal, so they tried to disguise an ox by hanging copper coins all over its body.

When the hunters handed over the fake unicorn, they were very nervous. But, when the inspector saw the strange animal he said with pleasure, "If it weren't for all the copper coins on its body, this beast would clearly be an ox."

50. 咸 鱼

从前，有一个对吃食过于吝啬的人，连儿子也舍不得给点好东西吃。一天吃饭时，桌上什么菜都没有。大孩子问："大①，有什么菜吗？"

那人说："有，墙上挂的咸鱼就是菜。你俩看一眼咸鱼，就②一口饭。"

忽然间，弟弟大声嚷道："哥吃一口饭，看了好几次咸鱼。"

那人恨恨地说："咸死他！"

注 释

① 大：方言，父亲。 (Dialect) father.

② 就：菜饭搭配着吃。 (Have vegetables, or meat) to go with (rice).

50. Salted Fish

There was once a man, who was excessively frugal about food. He did not even give any good food to his sons. One day for dinner they had rice and not even one dish of meat or vegetables appeared on the table. The elder boy said, "Pa, are we having any other dishes?"

"Yes, of course, why the salted fish hanging on the wall is a dish," said the father, "You can have a mouthful of rice and look once at the salted fish."

Suddenly the younger brother yelled, "Pa, elder brother had a mouthful of rice and looked at the salted fish several times."

"Let him die of salt, then." said the man resentfully.

51. 笑考官

从前，有一个穷书生将一只鹅送给考官。考官半嗔①半喜地说："如果受了你的鹅，我没有东西喂它，鹅就要饿死；如果谢绝你的礼物，我就有失礼貌。这叫我怎么办才好？"

书生说："大人，恕我直言。饿死鹅是小事，失礼可是大事！"

考官说："却之不恭，受之有愧。那我只好收下了！"

注 释

① 嗔：有生气、责怪之意。 Be angry and blame.

51. Laughing at the Chief Examiner

Once upon a time a poor scholar gave a goose to the chief examiner, who pretended to be half-annoyed and half-pleased.

"If I receive your goose, I won't have anything to feed it. The goose is going to die of hunger, isn't it?" the chief examiner said. "If I refuse your gift, I'm impolite. I don't know what I should do."

The scholar said, "Your Excellency, may I be so bold as to say it is a minor matter to let a goose die of hunger, but it's a major matter to be impolite."

"To decline would be disrespectful while to accept is embarrassing," said the examiner. "Then I have to accept it."

52. 属 牛

从前，有个县令要过生日，因为他属鼠，因此大家凑钱，专门铸了一只黄金老鼠，呈献县官，作为生日的贺礼。

县令接受了这件贵重礼物，非常高兴，又对送礼的人们说："你们知不知道我夫人的生日？她的生日也快到了。她比我小一岁，是属牛的。再送礼时，千万记住，牛肚里不要铸成空的！"

52. Born in the Year of the Ox

The story goes that a county magistrate was celebrating his birthday. Since he was born in the year of the mouse, some people collected money and gave him a golden mouse as a birthday present.

Accepting the valuable present, the magistrate was very pleased and said to the people, "Do you know when my wife's birthday is? Her birthday is nearly here too. She's one year younger than I, born in the year of the Ox. So when you present the gift to her you want to be sure to remember not to cast the ox with an empty belly!"

53．最凉快的地方

有一年夏天非常炎热，几位官老爷在一起商议着公事。大家热得受不了，其中一位官老爷提出换一处凉快的地方。

有人说："河边的亭子里很凉快。"

又有人说："庙里的大殿上更凉快。"

旁边的老百姓听到他们的谈论后，齐声说："大老爷们要想凉快，小民们知道最凉快的地方。"

官老爷们忙问："在什么地方？"

百姓说："老爷们的大堂里最凉快。"

众官惊问："那儿既无山又无水，怎么会最凉快呢？"

百姓巧妙地回答：“那里是不见天日的地方，阴森森的，怎么不风凉？”

53. The Coolest Place

One summer it was very, very hot. Some bureaucrats were discussing official duties, but they couldn't bear such hot weather. One bureaucrat suggested that they should change their meeting place for a cooler one.

Another one said at once, "It is nice and cool in the pavillion by the river."

Another said, "It is cooler in the main hall of the Buddhist temple."

Some common people nearby heard their discussion, and said in chorus, "You lords want to be cool, we know the coolest place of all."

"Where?" the bureaucrats asked hastily.

"The coolest place is right in your government hall," the common people answered.

"There is neither hill nor river here. Why is it the coolest place?" they asked surprised.

"There is neither sky nor sun, and it's very gloomy. How can it not be the coolest place of all?" the common people answered cleverly.

54. 背着客人吃饭

有一位主人让客人在厅堂里坐着，而他却悄悄地溜进里面吃饭。客人觉察到这事，故意大声说："这房间多么漂亮啊！可惜屋梁都被虫子蛀空了！"

主人听到了，急忙跑出来问道："虫子在哪里？"

客人一语双关地说："它在里面吃，外面怎么能知道呢？"

54. Having a Meal Behind the Guest's Back

Once a host let his guest sit in the sitting-room and he himself quietly slipped into the kitchen to have a meal. The guest became aware of what happened, and intentionally said aloud, "How beautiful the room is! What a pity many roof beams are being eaten away by worms!"

The host heard this and rushed out. "Where?" he asked.

"They eat on the inside, so from the outside you can't tell." the guest replied cunningly.

55. 草　书①

一位张丞相②很喜欢草书，但并不下功夫练。大家都讥笑他的书法不佳，丞相倒也毫不在意。

一天，他偶然拟得一佳句，立即挥毫疾书，可谓是满纸龙蛇飞舞。写罢，他令侄儿誊写一遍。

当侄儿动手抄写时，瞠目结舌，无从下笔。他只得拿着手稿去问丞相：“伯父，我不认识您写的字。请告诉我这是些什么字？”

丞相反复地看了许久，连自己也不认识，便责备侄儿说：“你为什么不早来问我？到现在我也忘记写了些什么！”

注 释

① 草书：汉字字体的一种，笔画相连，书写较快。这里是指字迹潦草。 A kind of Chinese writing style with strokes connected and written quickly. Here it indicates sloppy handwriting.

② 丞相：中国古代职位最高的大臣。 A minister who is in the highest position below the emperor in ancient China.

55. A Cursive Hand

Prime Minister Zhang was fond of handwriting, but he didn't put in a lot of effort to do his exercises. Everybody sneered at his bad handwriting, and the Prime Minister himself really didn't care.

One day he happened to draft a beautiful sentence and at once wielded his writing brush to write it down, indeed, there were dragons flying and snakes dancing all over the paper. Then he ordered his nephew to copy it.

When beginning to copy, his nephew stared tongue-tied and did not know where to start.

The young man had to take the manuscript back to the Prime Minister.

"Uncle, I can't read your handwriting, please tell me what words they are."

The Prime Minister read his cursive hand a long time, and did not know what Chinese characters they were, either. He then turned to blame his nephew. "Why didn't you come earlier to ask me? I myself have forgotten the words which I've written."

56. 好卖弄的人

有一个好卖弄的人，与儿子一同在大街上行走。迎面来了一个朋友，不认识他的儿子，便问："这位青年是谁？"

那人得意洋洋地大声说："他虽是朝廷宠臣吏部尚书的外孙的第九代的嫡亲①女婿，却是我的儿子。"

注 释

① 嫡亲：指在封建宗法制下的家庭正支。 Blood relations, especially paternal relations of a family under the clan system in the feudal society

56. Showing off

A man was fond of showing off. One day he went for a walk in the street with his son. On the way they came across a friend who didn't know his son and asked, "And who is this young man?"

The man replied with an air of complacency, "He is a blood relative of the son-in-law of the ninth generational grandson of the favorite Minister of Interior in the imperial court, that is; my son."

57. 凑不起

某朝代，一位书生正在参加科举考试，苦苦构思，难以成章。他的书童①在考场门口守候多时。他整个下午见许多考生完卷离去。直至黄昏，书生仍未出来，家中又派一仆人来看看。

仆人问书童："作一篇文章不知要多少字？"

书童回答："不过五、六百字。"

仆人又问："难道少主人腹中竟没有五、六百字？"

书童宽慰他说："不要心急，他腹中五、六百字是有的，只是一时凑不起来罢了！"

注　释

① 书童：侍候主人读书兼做杂役的童仆。　A child servant who had to serve the master by reading and doing other odd jobs.

57. Can't Bring Together

In a certain dynasty a scholar was taking the imperial examination, and he thought the essay very hard to finish. His pageboy was waiting for the young master at the gate of the examination hall. All afternoon he saw many examiners who had handed their papers in at the gate while leaving. By dark, the scholar still hadn't come out. A servant from his home was sent to see what the matter was.

"How many characters is the essay to be composed of?" the servant asked the pageboy.

"Not over five or six hundred," said the boy.

"Hasn't our young master learnt by heart five or six hundred characters?"

"Don't worry about it! He has certainly learnt five or six hundred, it's just that he can't bring them all together at once." The pageboy said comfortingly.

58. 画 像

有一个画师从没有人请他画过像。有人劝他画一幅他夫妻的写真①，挂在门外，这样就能让众人了解，招徕顾客。

那画师如法照做。一天，他的泰山②来看望他们小夫妻，见门外墙上挂着的画像，问道："那位女子是谁？"

画师回答："她是你的女儿。"

这位老泰山听了，生气地说："她为什么和这个陌生男人坐在一起？"

注 释

① 写真：人像画。 Portrait.

② 泰山：岳父的尊称。 Respectful form of address for father-in-law.

58. Drawing a Portrait

There was once a painter, who had never been asked to draw portraits. Someone suggested that he should draw a portrait of his wife and himself and hang it on the front door, in this way other people would see it and he could solicit customers.

The painter did so according to the suggestion. One day his father-in-law came to see them, seeing the portrait, he asked, "Who is the woman?"

"She's your daughter," answered the painter.

"Why is she sitting beside that unfamiliar man?" said the father-in-law angrily.

59. 胡子稍微象一点

从前，一位画师画完一幅画像，对他的主顾说：鄙人①虽非丹青妙手②，但也不是平庸之辈。请阁下③邀人来评议您的写真，便知分晓。”

主顾采纳了他的意见，请了一些人评论画像。

第一位说：“方顶帽画得相当象。”

第二位说：“衣服也很象。”

画师急忙插嘴：“帽子和衣服不是主要的，请对面容发表意见。”

第三位把画像与本人端详再三，然后只得尬尴地说：“胡子稍微象一点。”

注　释

① 鄙人：自己的谦称。 Self-depreciatory way to refer to oneself.

② 丹青妙手：丹青指红色和青色的颜料，丹青妙手指画艺高超的画家。丹 means red and 青 means green. The phrase refers to a great painter.

③ 阁下：敬称对方。 A very respectful way to address one's listener.

59. The Beard Is Somewhat Alike

An artist once finished painting a portrait, and said to his client, "Although my painting hasn't the superb touch of a great painter, it isn't mediocre. Ask anyone to discuss it with you and I'm sure you'll hear the same result."

The client accepted the suggestion and asked the opinions of some other people.

"The flattop cap is quite similiar." said the first guest.

"The clothes are very similiar, too," said the second one.

The artist hurriedly interrupted, "The cap and clothes aren't important. Please give some opinions on the facial features."

The third one compared the portrait with the client himself again and again, then ackwardly said, "The beard is somewhat alike."

60. 撒酒疯

从前，有一个人不管饮酒多少，总要撒酒疯。他的妻子恨透他这个毛病。

一天，他在家又要饮点酒了。妻子有意递给他一碗酸辣汤当酒。饮后不久，他又手舞足蹈起来。

妻子大声喝道："该死的！你喝的什么？那是酸辣汤，你还撒什么酒疯！"

那人笑道："我说呢，今天酒疯撒不起劲头来。"

60. Drunk and Crazy

Once upon a time there was a man who didn't care how much he drank as long as he got drunk and crazy. His wife despised this shortcoming.

One time while at home and as usual eager to drink, his wife purposely passed him a bowl of hot and sour soup and soon he started dancing for joy.

"Be damned! What the hell you drinking?" his wife yelled, "That's hot and sour soup, what kind of crazy drunkeness is this?"

"I'll tell you," the man said laughing: "Today my vigour acted without the spirit of the wine."

61. 难道你还要等上菜吗?

一次，一个老头同儿子抬着一罐酒。在路上，父子俩滑倒了，罐子被打破了，酒淌了满地。老头正在生气，却见儿子趴在地上。

老头问："你在干什么？"

儿子说："爹，多美的酒啊！我可要喝个够。来一块喝呀！难道你还要等上菜吗？"

61. Waiting for Food

An old man and his son once carried a pot of wine. Along the way they both slipped and fell, breaking the pot and spilling wine everywhere. The old man himself, was upset; but suddenly saw his son lying prone on the ground.

"What are you doing?" asked the old man.

"Dad, what good wine! I'll drink my fill, come drink with me! Don't tell me you're waiting for the food to come."

62. 好运气

某人去看望朋友，在途中被狗咬伤了腿。他疼痛极了，低头看见腿上流了不少血。

那人喜出望外地说："好运气！今天我幸亏没有穿长袜子。"

62. Good Luck

A man was once bit on the leg by a dog while going to see his friend. He was in great pain and bent down to see that his leg was bleeding profusely.

"What luck!" said the man overjoyed, "Fortunately, I'm not wearing stockings today!"

63. 再大便一次

从前，一个农夫不懂礼貌。一天，他进城买东西，竟在县衙门前随地大便，被人扭送见官。

官员问："你愿挨打，还是愿受罚？"

农夫害怕打板子①，回答道："愿意受罚。"

"那么，罚一两半银子。"

农夫拿出一块银子说："我这银子是三两，等我去截下一半，再来交罚款行吗？"

官员说："先把银子交上！"他接过银子，掂了掂，就和颜悦色地说："银子不找还你了！三两正好罚两次，准许你明天来这里再大便一次！"

注　释

① 打板子：打臀部，旧时一种刑法。 Beat one's behind, a kind of punishment in the old times.

63. One More Shit

There once was a farmer who had no understanding of common manners. One day when he was in town shopping, he carelessly took a shit in front of the county government office, and was caught and turned over to an official.

"Do you prefer to be beaten or fined?" asked the official.

The farmer was afraid to be beaten on the buns, and replied, "I'm willing to be fined."

"Then I fine you one and half *liang* (75 grams) of silver."

The farmer took out a piece of silver, and said, "This is three *liang*. Let me change it, and then I'll pay the fine, o.k.?"

"Hand it over to me first," the official said, receiving the piece of silver and weighing it in his hand. "It isn't necessary to get change, I say, the three *liang* is just the right amount for two shits. Tomorrow, I promise, you can come and take another shit." he said pleasantly.

64. 岂有此理

有个人喜欢学别人说话。一天，在回家路上，他听到人说“岂有此理”这四个字，他非常喜欢，就一路上“岂有此理，岂有此理”地念个不停。

后来他乘渡船过河时，因为忙乱，把这四个字忘了，便绕着船寻找。

船夫注意到那人的举动，问道：“你在找什么？”

那人回答：“是一句话。”

船夫说："话还有丢了的？真是岂有此理！"

那人一听，高兴地说："哈哈，'岂有此理'被你拾到了，为什么不早告诉我？"

64. That's Really Outrageous!

A man liked to follow what others said. One day on his way home he heard someone say the phrase, "That's really outrageous". He liked it very much and repeated it again and again while walking.

While hurrying to get on the ferry to cross a river, he suddenly forgot the phrase. He looked for it all around the boat.

A boatman noticed what the man was doing, and asked, "What are you looking for?"

"A pet phrase," the man answered.

"A phrase can't get lost" the boatman said. "That's really outrageous!"

"Aha!, you have picked it up," said the man happily, "why didn't you tell me earlier?"

65. 不吃素

某大户请了一个和尚① 念经超度② 亡母。主人准备第一顿饭菜时，想到和尚是从不开荤的，便问和尚："长老，您喝酒吗？"

那和尚说："你是知道的，酒嘛，倒能喝少许，但我唯独不吃素！"

注 释

① 和尚：出家修行的男佛教徒，终身吃素。 The male Buddhist who has to be a vegetarian all his life.

② 超度：指做佛事使（亡者的）灵魂脱离苦难。
Indicating the Buddhist service by which the soul of the dead could be saved from suffering.

65. Not a Vegetarian

A rich family once asked a Buddhist monk to recite scriptures for their late mother. While preparing the first meal, the host thought the monk never ate meat, therefore he asked, "Elder, would you like a drink?"

"As you know, I can drink only a little," said the monk. "And I don't only eat vegetables."

66．说话灵活

从前，一个买卖人教儿子说话要灵活些，不要把话说死。恰好此时有邻居来借几件用品。那人对邻居说："对不起，我不知道有没有，让我找一找，过一会儿再告诉你。"

邻居走后，那人对儿子说："刚才我同邻居的对话就很灵活；不说有，也不说没有，模棱两可。你要学会这样说话的艺术。"

儿子记住了父亲的话。一天，有客来访。客人问："令尊在家吗？"

那孩子回答："对不起，我想有的在家，有的出去了。让我进去看一看，过一会儿再告诉你。"

66. Talk Flexibly

Once upon a time a businessman was teaching his son how to talk flexibly, and not stiffly. Just then a neighbour came to borrow a few articles of daily use. The man said to the neighbour, "I'm sorry I don't know whether we have them or not. Let me have a look, after a while I'll tell you."

When the neighbour left, the man said to his son, "Just now my talk with the neighbour was very flexible. I didn't say yes and I didn't say no, it's all very equivocal. You must learn the art of talking like this."

The boy kept his father's instruction in mind. One day a visitor called on the man.

"Is your father in?" the visitor asked.

"I'm sorry, I think some are in and some are out. Let me go in and have a look, after a while I'll let you know," the boy replied.

67. 麻雀请客

一天，麻雀请鹦鹉和鹰吃饭。排座次时，麻雀首先对鹦鹉说："您的衣冠很华丽，自然要请在上席坐。"

麻雀转身白了鹰一眼，说："你穿得寒酸，只好屈你在下席了。"

鹰恼怒地嚷道："你这个小人①，怎么长着一双这样势利的眼啊！"

麻雀坦坦然道："世上有谁不知道我的心眼儿小，目光如豆。"

注 释

① 小人：指品德卑劣的人。 Person with a mean personality.

67. A Sparrow Invites Guests to Dinner

One day a sparrow invited a parrot and an eagle to dinner. As they were taking their seats, the sparrow first said to the parrot, "Your dress is so gorgeous! Please take the seat of honor."

The sparrow turned to the eagle in distain, "You are poorly dressed. I'm afraid you have to sit in the humble seat."

"You villain, how snobbish you are!" the eagle yelled angrily.

The sparrow replied calmly, "Everyone in the world knows my heart is small and I'm short-sighted."

68. 前面也有雨

从前，有个书呆子在大雨中慢慢行走。一个过路人问他："雨这么大，你为什么还这么慢腾腾地走？"

书呆子从容地回答说："快点儿走有什么用？前面也有雨。"

68. It's Raining down the Road Too

A bookworm was once walking slowly in the heavy rain. A passer-by asked, "Why are you walking so slowly in this heavy rain?"

"What's the use of hurrying?" the bookworm said leisurely, "when it's raining down the road too."

69. 吸气排烟

有个地主对仆人很刻薄，从不让人吃饱，也不付工钱，许多仆人都悻悻地离他而去。

有一个人捉摸透了他爱财如命的心理，假意地对他说："我探听到这么一个人，他可以不吃饭，也不要你的工钱。如你愿意，可以雇用他试试。"

地主问："一个人不吃饭，不会饿死吗？"

那人说："据说他曾遇到过一个神仙，学会了'吸气排烟'充饥方法，所以从来不吃东西。"

地主想了一会，说："那我也不想雇他。"

"为什么？"那人惊讶地问。

"光吸气不吃饭固然很合我的心意，但光排烟不大便，那我就少了一个人的粪肥田了！"

69. Drawing a Breath and Emptying Smoke

The story goes that a rich man was very mean to his servants. He never paid them nor gave them enough food. So many servants left him resentfully.

One of his friends saw through him and said pretendingly: "I have found a person who doesn't care about pay and has no need of food. If you like, try employing him."

"If one doesn't have meals, won't he die of hunger?" asked the rich man.

"People say the man has met a god, and learned the way of 'drawing a breath and emptying smoke' to appease hunger, therefore he never eats any food," answered the friend.

The rich man thought a while, "I don't think I want to hire him."

"Why?" the friend asked in surprise.

"It suits me fine that he only draws breath and doesn't eat, but he only exhales smoke and doesn't defecate. Well, in this way I'll be short of fertilizer to enrich the fields."

70. 三 斤[1]

有个糊涂县官嗜酒如命，整天喝得醉醺醺的。一天午后，他喝完一壶酒，正要叫人再买些来。忽然间，门外有人喊冤告状。这使他非常扫兴，所以一升堂就令衙役拿板子来，打喊冤的人。

衙役问："打[2]多少？"

县官伸出三个指头说："三斤。"

大堂上所有的人一时莫名其妙，随即便哄然放声大笑起来。

注 释

① 斤：计量单位，等于半公斤。A unit of measure equal to 0.5 kilogramme.

② 打：（一）打人，打板子；（二）买，如：打酒、打酱油。 (1) Beat, hit, e.g. 打人，打板子； (2) buy, ladle, e.g. 打酒，打酱油.

70. Three *Jin* of Wine

Once there was a county magistrate who was crazy about wine and not a day passed without getting drunk. One afternoon just as he had done away with a pot of wine and was about to order more; there was a cry in the street from a person demanding justice from being wronged. This greatly annoyed the magistrate and he ordered that this person be interrogated. Deciding to punish this person for crying of injustice, he asked the *yamen* runners to bring some birches.

"How many strokes?" a runner asked.

"Three *jin*," the leader said, stretching out his three fingers.

All the clerks and runners in the hall were at first puzzled, then burst out into uproarious laughter.

71. 刮地皮[1]

从前，有一个贪得无厌的地方官在任上千方百计搜刮了许多不义之财。当他任期已满，回到家中时，看见家属里多了一个老头儿。他惊奇地问道："你是谁？"

老头说："我是不久前你管辖地方的土地爷[2]。"

"你为什么走老远的路，到我家来？"

"那地方上的地皮都被你刮光了，我无处安身，叫我怎么能不跟你来呢？"

注 释

① 刮地皮：讽喻贪官搜刮民财。 An allegory referring to corrupt officials extorting money from the people.

② 土地爷：故事里常说的管辖一段地区的土地神。 The earth god in legend who was in charge of a certain area.

71. Razing the Ground

Long time ago, a very greedy official had extorted a lot of ill-gotten wealth. Having finished his term of office, he returned home and saw a strange old man among his relatives. "Who are you?" he asked surprisedly.

"I am the Earth God of the county that was, until not long ago, ruled by you," the old man said.

"Why have you walked such a long way to come here to my home?"

"The ground of my county has been razed by you, I could not find a place to stay. What could I do but come here with you?"

72. 七 月 儿

从前，一位妇女怀孕七个月，生下一个婴儿。她的丈夫担心小孩长不大，逢人就问有关早产婴儿的事。

一天，他又与朋友提起这事。朋友劝他说："你何必过虑，我祖父也是不足七个月出生的。"

那人迫不及待地问："我很想知道你祖父是否长大了？"

72. A Baby Born Within Seven Months

Once upon a time a woman gave birth to a baby after being pregnant for seven months. Her husband was afraid the baby wouldn't grow up, so he asked whoever happened to come his way about it.

One day he talked it over again with one of his friends. "Don't worry," the friend advised him. "My grandfather was born within seven months, too."

The man, unable to hold himself back, said, "I wonder whether your grandfather grew up later on."

73. 头皮薄

某理发匠替一个老者剃光头。他手艺差，刚下手便在老人头上割了几道口子，只得停住剃刀。

理发匠说："您老人家头皮太薄，难下剃刀。待一些日子，您老的头皮长厚了，再找我剃头吧！"

73. The Thin Skin of the Head

A young barber once was shaving an old man's head. Being unskilled, he soon made many cuts in several places on the old man's head right after he started.

"Granddad, the skin of your head is too thin for my razor," said the barber. "Please wait a few days and let me shave your head again after your skin gets thicker.

74. 告饥荒

有一年，农村发生灾荒，农夫向官府报告灾情，请求免去赋税。县官问前来报荒的老翁：“今年麦收了多少？”

老翁答：“三成。”

县官又问：“棉花收了多少？”

答：“两成。”

县官再问：“稻子收了多少？”

答：“也两成。”

县官发怒道：“有七成年景，你还捏造什么荒情？”

老翁说：“我今年一百四十多岁了，实在没有见过这样的特大饥荒。”

县官听后，益发大怒，训斥老汉虚报年龄。

老翁不慌不忙地说：“我今年七十多，大儿四十，小儿三十，合起来不正好一百四十多岁了？”

这一番话，引起一阵哄堂大笑。

74. Reporting Famine Conditions

One year the countryside was struck by famine. Farmers went to the local officials to report the conditions of the famine and to ask for tax exemptions.

"How much wheat have you harvested this year?" a local official asked an old man who had come to report.

"30%," answered the old man.

"How about cotton?"

"20%."

"And rice?"

"20%, as well."

"That makes 70% of the year's harvest, what kind of fabricated famine report is this?" the official said angrily.

"I'm now over one hundred and forty. I have never seen such an extraordinarily serious famine."

The official was now in a greater rage and scolded him for lying about his age.

"Well," said the old man calmly, "I'm older than seventy, but my elder son is forty and my younger son is thirty; that adds up to over one hundred and forty, doesn't it?"

At that, the whole hall rocked with laughter.

75. 饼 钱

一个人到一家小吃店，问一个饼卖多少钱？店掌柜说："一个饼卖一个铜钱。"那人吃完了几个饼，如数付了钱。

掌柜说："饼不用面粉吗？应给面钱。"

那人说："对！"说罢，付了面钱。

掌柜又说："饼需用烧柴呀？应加柴费。"

"对！"那人说罢，又付了柴费。

"饼靠师傅做出来的，对吗？应加上工夫钱。"

"对！"那人说罢，再添上工夫钱。

在回家路上，他感到有点不对味儿，自言自语说："我够蠢的！我给了面钱，柴费和工资，店掌柜不该还要我的饼钱啊！"

75. The Cost of Pancakes

A man once entered a snack bar, and asked how much a cake was. The shopkeeper said that one cake cost one copper cash. The man ate up a few pancakes and paid the exact number in coins.

"Doesn't the pancake need flour? You have to pay for the flour," the shopkeeper said.

"Right," said the man, giving him some money for the flour.

"And aren't the pancakes cooked with firewood? You should pay me for that."

"Right," the man said, handing money over for the firewood.

"The pancakes are made by the cook, aren't they? The wages have to be paid all the same."

"Yes, of course," the man said, adding a few coins for the cook's wages.

On the way home, the man thought something wasn't quite right. "How stupid I am! I paid him money for the the flour, firewood and wages," the man said to himself, "so the shopkeeper shouldn't have asked me to pay for the pancakes."

76.咸　蛋

有一次，甲和乙在一起吃咸蛋，甲惊异说："我往常吃的蛋都是淡的，今天吃的这个蛋为什么这么咸？"

乙也不清楚是什么原因，但是他愣充内行，得意洋洋地解释说："幸亏你问我，咸蛋，也就是咸鸭子下的蛋嘛！"

76. Salted Eggs

A and B once were eating salted eggs together. A was surprised and said, "The eggs that I've eaten before were not salty at all. Why are today's eggs so salty?"

"Luckily you asked me the question," B, not knowing the reason either, but pretending to be an expert, explained proudly, "The salted eggs, well, they were laid by salted ducks!"

77. 我逃到哪里去了？

一个和尚犯了法，被差役押去充军。一天他们在途中一个客栈里过夜，和尚以烧酒款待差役，把差役灌醉了。和尚乘机把差役的头发剃得光光的，然后急匆匆地逃跑了。

差役酒醒后，到处找不到和尚。后来偶然摸着了自己剃得光光的和尚头，便大叫起来：“和尚倒在这里，可是我逃到哪里去了？”

77. Where Have I Escaped to?

A Buddhist monk once committed a crime. He was banished, under the guard of a runner, to a distant army post. One night they put up in an inn, where the monk entertained the runner with strong drink. Soon the runner was drunk. The monk seized the opportunity to have the runner's head shaved and ran away.

After sobering up, the runner looked everywhere, but couldn't find the monk. Awhile later he accidentally touched his recently shaven head and burst out, "The monk is here! But where have I escaped to?"

78. 三十而立

清朝①一个教习②让两个学生写“三十而立”这篇文章的破题③。

一个学生磨蹭了半天，写道：在十五岁的两倍年龄，虽有椅子、板凳而不敢坐。

另一个学生则写道：年过花甲④的一半，只能直挺挺地站着。

注 释

① 清朝（1644—1911）：中国最后一个封建王朝。
The last feudal dynasty in China.

② 教习：教员。 Tutor, instructor.

③ 破题：八股文（科举考试的文体）的前两句，要求说破题目的意义。 Similar to a title sentence where the main thesis of the article is stated in the first two lines of a *baguwen* (the standard style of article in imperial examinations).

④ 花甲：指六十岁。 Sixty years old.

78. Achieving Success at the Age of Thirty

In the Qing Dynasty a teacher made two students write the starting lines of the essay, "Standing on One's Feet at Thirty".

After a long time one wrote: At the age of double fifteen, one dare not sit on the chair or the bench; the other wrote: At the age of half sixty, one can only stand erect.

79. 江湖医生①

从前，一个病人请医生看病。这个江湖医生信口开河，保证能治好他的病。他为治病花去大量的金钱，病却日见严重，最后停止了呼吸。

病人家属恨透这个江湖医生，便叫一个仆人前去辱骂。一会儿，仆人回来了，大家忙问他骂了没有？

仆人哭丧着脸说："医生门前骂的人太多，若轮到我，恐怕明天也挨不上号②！"

注 释

① 江湖医生：走街串巷行医的冒牌医生。 Itinerant quack doctor.

② 挨不上号：北方话，轮不上的意思。 (Northern dialect) can't get into one's turn.

79. A Quack Doctor

Once upon a time a patient went for a doctor, and the doctor shot off his mouth and promised a cure for the patient. He spent a lot of money on the treatment, but day by day his illness got worse and finally he died.

An extreme hatred developed between the sick person's family and the doctor, and they sent a servant to curse the doctor. After a while the servant returned, and everybody asked him whether he had cursed or not.

"There were many, many people cursing at the doctor's front door," the servant said, putting on a long face. "I'm afraid my turn won't come until tomorrow."

80. 五大天地

从前，一个官贪财好酒，胡作非为，百姓怨恨。到卸任时，公众送他一块德政匾①，上面写着“五大天地”四个大字。

那官兴高采烈地问：“这四个字是什么意思？”

众人齐声回答：“你到任时，金天银地；你在家时，花天酒地；坐堂断案，昏天黑地；百姓含冤，恨天怨地；你下台了，谢天谢地！”

注 释

① 德政匾：写着表彰官吏政绩题词的木牌。 A wooden board on which the merits of an official was inscribed.

80. The Five Big Heavens and Earths

The story goes that an official was fond of drink and money and committed all kinds of ou trageous acts. The people hated him. When he was relieved of his office, the public gave him a horizontal board with four Chinese characters inscribed on it, "The Five Big Heavens and Earths".

The official said in great delight, "What does it mean? I can hardly understand it."

The public said in chorus, "It means when taking office, you had a golden heaven and silver earth; when at home, you led a life of debauchery (lit. — heaven of flowers and earth of wine); when judging cases, total injustice prevailed (lit. — dark heaven and black earth); when the people suffered from wrong doing, discontent was heard all round (lit. — hatred in heaven and discontent on earth); when you left office, everybody thanked the heavens and earth."

81. 心在嘴上

一次，一位武术师教徒弟练拳，告诫与人交手时，不要打击对方的嘴。

徒弟不明其意，问道："为什么不要打对方的嘴？"

武术师解释说："按理胸部是最重要部位，因为它里面有心脏；但现时许多人整天把心放在嘴上，你若打他的嘴，他岂能活命？"

81. The Heart on the Mouth

Once a Chinese martial arts coach, while teaching his apprentice how to box, warned him not to hit his opponent on the mouth when coming to blows.

The apprentice didn't understand what the coach meant, and asked, "Why not hit the opponent on the mouth?".

"Ordinarily the chest is the most important part because that's where the heart is; but today so many fellows have their hearts in their mouths all day long," the coach said, "If you hit them on the mouth, how can it be that they are alive?"

82.换 针

出嫁前夕，一个闺女在房里收拾东西。她父亲从窗隙间往里瞧，听到女儿不断的喃喃低语。

“这几件衣服带去能穿好几年，那几件东西也该带走……”

这时，碰巧她父亲有几根胡子穿过了窗缝，被女儿一眼看见。她扯住胡子说：“这撮头发也带去，能换几根针使使。”

82. Change for Needles

On the eve of the wedding day, a daughter was packing up things in her room when her father peeped through the crack of the window and listened to his daughter murmuring.

"These dresses can be carried away to wear for years; those things also must go . . . . "

At this moment the father's beard appeared through the window paper. His daughter catching a glance of it went over and began pulling at it, saying, "I'll take these hairs too and change them for needles."

83.莫砍虎皮

从前，有个人被老虎叼去，他的儿子提着刀去追杀老虎，抢救父亲。

这人在虎口里大声喊：“儿啊，你想要杀死老虎，最好砍它的脚。千万莫砍虎皮！按目前时价，虎皮可值钱啊！”

83. Not to Cut Its Skin

A man was once held in the mouth of a tiger, his son ran after it with a knife and wanted to kill the wild animal to rescue his father from danger.

"My son, if you want to kill it, you'd better knife its paws." Yelled the man in the tiger's mouth. "Be sure not to cut its skin, as the tiger fur is worth a lot of money at current prices."

84. 出生太晚

某公①晚年丧妻，续娶了一个年轻的女子。新妇感到夫妻年龄不般配，每天郁郁不乐，眉头紧锁。

某公觉察到新妇的情况，问道："你是不是恨我年纪大？"

新妇回答："不是。"

"那么你嫌我官卑职小？"

"也不是。"

"那么，你每天愁容满面又为的什么！"

新妇说："不恨夫君②年纪大，不嫌夫君官职小；只恨我出生太晚，没能看到夫君年青时的俊模样。"

注 释

① 公：尊称中年以上的男子。 A respectful form of address for a man older than middle age.

② 夫君：丈夫。 Husband.

84. Born Too Late

Once a gentleman was bereft of his wife in old age, and was remarried to a young woman. His bride felt their age wasn't a right match. Everyday she knitted her brows unhappily.

The man discovering his bride's frame of mind, asked, "Do you have a hatred of my age?"

"No," the bride answered.

"Then do you dislike my low rank?"

"No, not that either."

"Then why do you look so extremely worried every day?"

"I hate neither your age nor your low rank, I only hate the fact that I was born too late to see with my own eyes the handsome looks of my husband's youth."

85. 补鞋窍门

从前，一个修鞋匠掌握了一种补鞋窍门。他永远只使用一双皮底。顾客修完鞋，走出他的铺子，那双补过的鞋底便会自动地掉下来。所以他总是跟在他的顾客后面，拾回皮底，留着下次用。

一天，他跟随在一位顾客后面，没有见到那双皮底掉下来，他慌得大声嚷道："我此生买卖可就完了！"

待他回到家中，发现那双皮底竟掉在自己铺子里的地面上。

85. Key to Mending Shoes

A shoe-repairer once had a key to mending shoes, he only used one pair of leather soles during his life. As soon as the customers stepped out of his shop, the mended pair of soles automatically fell out. So he always followed his customers, picked up the leather soles, and then used them on the next customer.

One day after following a customer, he couldn't find the leather soles, "For the first time in my life, my business is ruined!" he cried in alarm.

When he returned to the shop he saw the pair of leather soles on the floor.

86.属 蟒

某人问：“喂，老兄！你是属什么的？”

那人回答说：“我是属蟒的，今年五十五岁。”

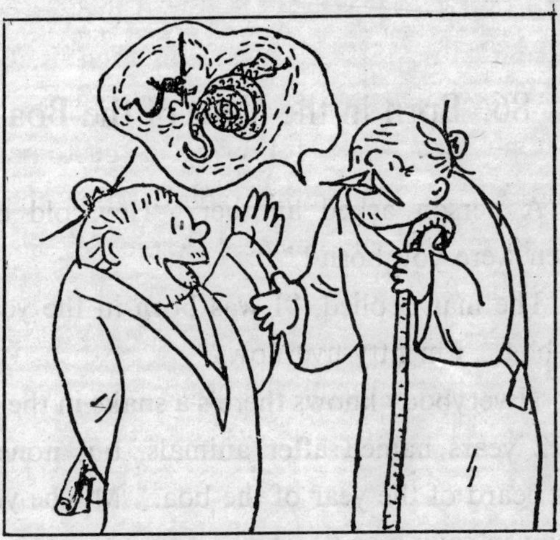

“大家都知道十二生肖①中只有蛇年，从没有人听说过蟒年，也许你说错了。”

那人笑说：“老弟，你讲得完全对，但我讲得也不错。毫无疑问，我是属蛇的，但是你想想，一条蛇活了五十五年，那怕是一条小蛇，也早该长成大蟒了。”

注 释

① 十二生肖：中国民间以十二种动物计算人的生年，称“十二生肖”，又称“属相”。 In China, twelve animals are usd to symbolize the year of one's birth, called 十二生肖 or 属相.

86. Born in the Year of the Boa

A person asked another, "Hey, old chap! When were you born?"

The man replied, "I was born in the year of the boa. I'm fifty-five now."

"Everybody knows there's a snake in the cycle of 12 years named after animals, but none has ever heard of the year of the boa. Maybe you're wrong in saying so."

"My boy, what you say is quite true, and what I said isn't untrue, either," said the man. "I was born in the year of the snake for sure. But if you think about it, a snake which has lived to be fifty-five must grow to be as big as a boa even if it was a little snake in it's early years."

87.懒女人

从前，有一个非常懒惰的女人，什么事都不愿做。如果没有现成饭，她宁可饿肚子。

有一次，她的丈夫要出门办事，怕她挨饿，临行前给她烙了一张特大的饼。丈夫把饼的中央剜空，将大饼套在她的脖子上，才放心地走了。

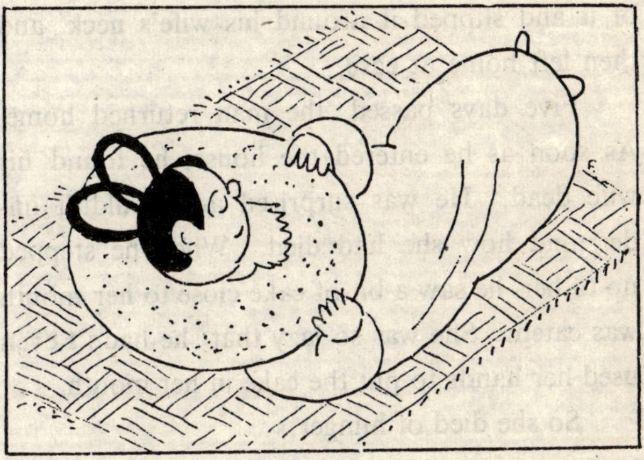

五天过后，丈夫回到家里。他开门一看，发现妻子已经死了。他大吃一惊，不明白妻子怎样会死的。待走近跟前一看，原来靠近她嘴边的饼只吃了一点，其余的她都懒得用手转到嘴边去吃，硬是活活给饿死了！

87. A Lazy Woman

There once was a woman who was very, very lazy, and would do nothing. If no one cooked for her, she would rather be hungry.

One day her husband was going out to do some business. Being afraid that she would suffer from hunger he baked a big cake, cut out the center of it and slipped it around his wife's neck, and then left home at ease.

Five days passed, the man returned home. As soon as he entered the house, he found his wife dead. He was surprised and couldn't understand how she had died. When he stepped up to her, he saw a bit of cake close to her mouth was eaten. She was so lazy that she hadn't even used her hands to put the cake in her mouth.

So she died of hunger.

88."哑巴"说话

有一个叫化子①，假装哑巴。他经常在大街上手指木碗，口里发出"咿咿哑哑"的声音，向人讨乞。

一天，他手里拿了两枚铜板②，进了酒店，对店家说："打点酒喝。"

店家吃惊地问："你平日在这街上往来，从来不会说话；今天你怎么开口说话了？"

叫化子说："平日我身无分文，叫我怎样张得开口？今天有了两个铜板，我自然有胆说话了。"

注 释

① 叫化子：口语，即乞丐。 (Colloq.) beggar.

② 铜板：又名铜钱。见111页注释。 Copper cash, also called 铜钱. See p.111.

88. The Dumb Can Speak

There was once a beggar who pretended to be dumb. He often pointed to a wooden bowl with his finger, made husky sounds of "ah, ah" and begged money from pedestrians in the streets.

One day, he held two copper cash in his hand and went to a wineshop. "Please sell me a little wine," the beggar said to the shopkeeper.

"You used to go around this street unable to speak. How can you speak today?" said the shopkeeper with astonishment.

"In those days I was flat broke, how could I open my mouth?" said the beggar. "Today I have two copper cash, naturally I have the courage to speak."

89. 一毛不拔①

一个猴子死后去见阎王爷②，求阎王爷让他来生投胎变人。

"如果你想要成为人，首先你得拔掉身上的猴毛。"阎王爷说罢，叫牛头马面③帮猴子拔毛。

才拔出一根猴毛，猴子就忍不住嚎叫："多么痛啊！快别拔了！"

阎王爷大笑说："瞧你这猴头！连一根猴毛也舍不得拔掉，怎做得成人？"

注 释

① 一毛不拔：成语，比喻非常吝啬。 (Idiom) very penurious.

② 阎王爷：佛教中称管理地狱的神，也叫阎罗王。
The god who is in charge of hell in Buddhism, also called 阎罗王.

③ 牛头马面：阎王手下的两个鬼卒。 Two ghosts under the god of hell, one with a head of an ox and the other with a face of a horse.

89. Unwilling to Lose Even One Hair

A monkey went to see the King of Hell after having died, and begged the King to allow him to become a man in the next life.

"If you want to be a man, first you must pull out all the hair on your body," the King said, ordering two goblins to help the monkey pull his hairs.

As soon as the goblins began to pull out one hair, the monkey cried loudly and impatiently, "It hurts, it hurts! Stop pulling, please."

"Look, what a monkey! You are unwilling to lose even one hair, how will you ever become a man?" the King said, laughing a hearty laugh.

90. 偷 绳

从前，一个人因偷盗被罚游街示众。在大街上，他的一个朋友看见了，走上前问：“这是怎么一回事？”

那人说：“唉，倒霉！前天我在街上闲逛时，看见地上有一根绳子。我想那条绳子日后也许有用处，便顺手将它拾回家去。”

朋友说：“这点小事，为何处罚你这么重？”

那人回答说：“因为我没有看见绳子那头还拴着一头牛。”

90. Stealing a Rope

A man once was punished and paraded through the streets before the public for stealing. One of his friends caught a glimpse of him and came up to him.

"What's the matter with you?" asked the friend.

"Oh, bad luck! The day before yesterday while I was walking about in the street, I saw a rope on the ground," said the man. "I thought that the rope might be useful sometime in the future, so I picked it up and brought it home."

"Why did they punish you so severely for such a petty thing?" said the friend.

"Because I didn't see that there was a cow at the other end of the rope," answered the man.

91. 谈 猴

从前，一个长得瘦小的县官进见某大臣。他们谈完公事后，便闲谈起来。

大臣问："听说贵县①山上有猴子，不知道有多大？"

县官回答："大的猴子同大人②您差不多大小。"说完后，他觉察到自己无意中冒犯了大臣，惊恐万分。他立即离座躬身补充说："小猴子比卑职③我还要瘦小。"

注 释

① 贵县：尊称"您的"口语为"贵"，如贵姓，贵国。 Your honourable county, a respectful form of address.

② 大人：旧时称比自己地位高的官长。 Used to address one's superior in the old times.

③ 卑职：下级对上级官员的自称。 Used by an inferior referring to himself when speaking to his superior.

91. A Small Talk About Monkeys

Once upon a time a thin, small magistrate called on a minister, when finishing the discussion about affairs, they began having a small chat.

"I hear there are monkeys in the mountains of your country. I wonder how big they are," asked the minister.

"Some are almost as big as Your Excellency," the magistrate replied. With this word he realized he had made an indiscreet remark, so he was alarmed and panic-stricken.

"Some are thinner and smaller than I, your humble servant." he added, leaving his seat at once and bending himself slightly.

92.酸 酒

旧时，一家酒店的招牌上写着：“酒每斤八个铜钱；醋每斤十个铜钱”。一天，有两位顾客进店饮酒，而酒味很酸。其中一位皱眉头说：“好酸的酒啊！莫不是错拿了醋给我们？”

他的同伴急忙地踢他的脚说：“傻瓜，莫大声嚷嚷！瞧，招牌上写明醋比酒贵着哩！”

92. Sour Wine

In the past, the signboard of a wineshop read "Eight cash for one *jin* of wine; ten cash for a *jin* of vinegar". One day two men went for a drink in the shop. The wine was very sour. One of them frowned and said, "How sour the wine is! Was the vinegar given to us by mistake?"

His friend hastily kicked his feet under the table. "Fool, don't make so much noise!" he said in a whisper. "Look at the signboard, the vinegar is more expensive than the wine!"

93.润　肺

一个人举行茶话会，其中一位客人独自吃光了一盘核桃。

主人问："你为什么光吃核桃？"

客人回答："多吃核桃能润肺。"

主人拉下脸说："你只顾润自己的肺，就不管我的心疼①吗？"

注 释

① 心疼：此处为双关语。字面上以"心疼"对应"润肺"，因汉语"心疼"有"吝惜""舍不得"之意，实为讥讽主人吝啬。 Used as a matching word to 润肺，心疼 here is a pun in Chinese that also means "begrudge", mocking the host as a miser.

93. Nourishing the Lungs

There was once a man who was giving a tea party, and saw one of the guests eat nearly a whole plate of walnuts by himself.

"Why do you eat only the walnuts?" asked the host.

"Eating walnuts can nourish the lungs," the guest replied.

The host pulled a long face. "You are entirely absorbed in nourishing your lungs, but you don't care about my heartache."

94.不吉利话

一个儿童爱说不吉利的话。一天，他家的亲戚举行婚礼，他的父亲想领他前去贺喜。行前，父亲反复叮嘱他不要说不吉利的话。

那儿童对父亲的教导全当耳边风，不耐烦地说："爸爸，你别担心！我都十几岁了，还不知道喜事不同于丧事。"

在亲戚家，那儿童果然彬彬有礼，他父亲很高兴。告别主人时，那儿童却突然说："今天我可没说一句话，以后他们新郎新娘闹离婚，可别怪我！"

94. Unlucky Words

A child enjoyed saying unlucky things. One day there was a relative's wedding and his father wanted to take him to celebrate the happy event. Before going, the father repeatedly told him not to say anything unlucky.

The father's instruction went in one ear and out the other. "Don't worry, father! I'm already ten. I know a wedding isn't like a funeral," the child said impatiently.

In the relative's house, the child was refined and courteous, his father felt very delighted. When they took leave of their host, the child said suddenly, "Today I haven't said a word, so if the newlyweds divorce later on, don't blame me!"

95.高帽子[①]

有两个门生[②]即将赴外地做官，相约同去向座师[③]辞别。

座师告诫说："当今世风日下，喜欢阿谀奉承，总给上司送高帽子戴，你们应引以为戒。"

其中一个门生说："恩师[④]说得极是。当今世上，象恩师这样不喜欢戴高帽子的人，实在找不到几个啊！"

座师听后，面有喜色。

两个门生辞别出门，一人即对同伴说："你已经顺利地送了一顶高帽子给恩师戴上啦！"

注 释

① 高帽子：俗称奉承别人为戴高帽子。 (Colloq.) flattery.

② 门生：旧科举考试成名的考生拜主考官门下，成为该考官门下的学生。 Those who had passed the imperial examination acknowledged the chief official in charge of the examination as their teacher and became his students.

③ 座师：旧科举成名的考生对主考官的敬称。 Respectful address for the chief official in charge of the examination.

④ 恩师：敬称授业或栽培自己的老师。 Respectful address for one's teacher or trainer.

95. Flattery

There were once two graduates who were assigned to be officials in other provinces. They went together to bid farewell to their teacher.

The teacher exhorted them and said, "Nowadays the world is declining in its moral values.

Many people like to flatter and tip their hats to superiors. You should take warning from this."

One of the graduates replied, "Right! Our teacher's words are completely true. Today few men have a dislike for flattery as our teacher does!"

The teacher was much pleased with the graduate's talk.

After the two graduates took their leave, one said to his companion, "You've successfully flattered our teacher."

96.生豆腐

有一个老翁很富有，但极其吝啬。他每日三餐不备菜肴，仅以筷子蘸盐水下饭。

旁人对他说："令郎①在外嫖赌、吃喝，而你却过这样清苦的日子，值得吗？"

老翁发狠地说："从现在起，每顿饭我也要吃一块生豆腐，美美地享用一番。"

注 释

① 令郎：敬称对方的儿子。 Respectful address for another's son.

96. Uncooked Bean Curd

Once upon a time there was an old man who was very rich, but extremely stingy. For his daily three meals he never ate any meat or vegetables, but used his chopsticks to dip a little saltwater on his rice.

Someone said to him, "While you are so frugal, your son is out whoring, gambling, feasting, and drinking — is it worth leading such a dog's life?"

"From now on, then, I'll have a piece of uncooked bean curd at meals," the old man said with scorn, "and I'll enjoy it very much."

97.好好先生

东汉①有一个叫司马②徽的人，从不说人家的短处，同人交谈，不管好事坏事、喜事丧事、乐事愁事都说好。

有人问他身体如何？他回答“好”。

一次，一个朋友悲伤地告诉他，自己的儿子死了，他听了后，照样回答说：“很好，很好！”

妻子责备他：“人家认为你有高尚品德，所以才来相告家事。你为什么听到人家儿子死了，也说‘很好，很好’呢？”

司马徽说：“你说的话，也是很好的呀！”

现在人们称从不得罪人的人为好好先生，便来源于这个故事。

注 释

① 东汉（25—220）：中国早期封建朝代，也叫后汉。

An early feudal dynasty in China, also called 后汉.

② 司马：复姓。 A double-character surname.

97. A Yes Man

In the Eastern Han Dynasty (25 — 220) there was a person called Sima Hui, who never talked about other's shortcomings. In conversation with others, he always said "good" or "well" or "right", no matter whether it was good or bad, fortunate or unfortunate, happy or unhappy.

If someone asked him how he was, he replied "fine".

One day a friend of his came to him and said "I've come here to tell you some sad news, my son is dead." He said, "Very good, very good!"

His wife reproached him, "Your friend considered you noble, so he came to tell you the news of his son's death. Upon hearing the unhappy news, why did you say, 'very good'?"

Sima Hui said, "According to reason, your remark is very good, too."

Today people call those who never offend others a "Yes Man", which originates from this story.

98.醉 汉

一个醉汉梦见有人请他喝酒，他嫌酒凉，叫佣人拿酒去暖热。这时，他突然从梦中醒来。

他懊悔万分，自言自语地说："早知如此，何不就将那凉酒喝了呢！"

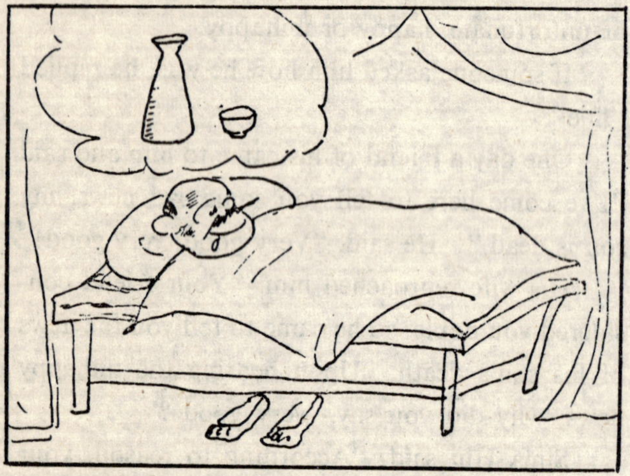

98. A Drunkard

One day a drunkard dreamed somebody was entertaining him to drink. He disliked cold wine, and ordered a servant to warm it. He suddenly awoke at this moment, and felt very remorseful.

"If I'd known I was going to wake up, I would have had that drink of cool wine," he grumbled to himself.

99.你把胡子挪到哪里去?

一天，口、鼻、眼、眉在一起争功摆好。

口对鼻说："你有什么能耐①，竟长在我的上面？"

鼻说："我能分别香臭，然后你方能张口饮食，所以我理应在你的上面。"

鼻转身对眼说："你有什么本事，敢占据我上面的位置？"

眼说："我能看东西，识别美丑，功劳不小，当然应该在你之上。"

鼻愤愤不平地说："就算你说得对。但眉毛有什么了不起，也高居我的上面？"

眉笑着说："我不同你争辩，我要是在你下面，你把胡子挪到哪里去？"

注 释

① 能耐：能力。北方口语。 (Northern dialect) ability.

99. Where Would You Move the Moustache?

One day the mouth, nose, eyes, and brows got together and enumerated their merits.

The mouth said to the nose, "What ability do you have? Why are you over me?"

The nose answered, "I can make a distinction between a sweet and a bad smell, then you can open your mouth and eat or drink, so my position should be over yours."

The nose turned to the eyes and said, "What about you eyes? Why are you above me?"

"I can see everything, and distinguish the beautiful and the ugly," said the eyes. "My contribution is bigger than yours, so I should be above you."

"Granted you are right," the nose said indignantly. "And how about you brows? Why are you above me, too?"

The brows said smiling, "I don't want to argue with you. But if I was under you, where would you move the moustache?"

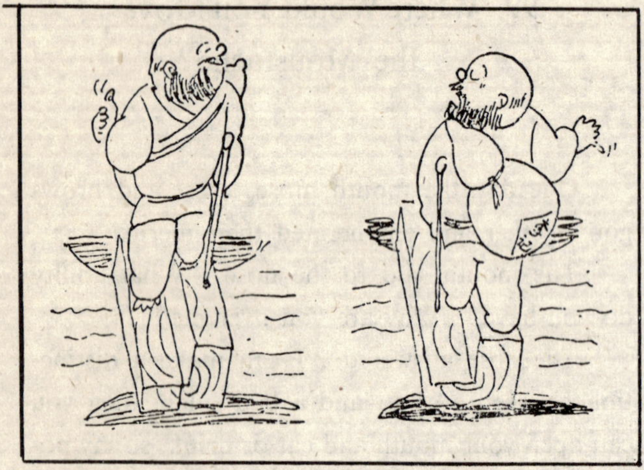

100.铁拐李①过桥

神仙铁拐李有一次过一座小桥。这桥用厚薄不同的两块木头搭成，桥面一边高，一边低。铁拐李瘸，一腿长，一腿短，所以走在桥上稳稳当当，他称赞说："这是人间最好的一座桥。

当他回来的时候，重过这座桥。因为方向相反，瘸腿正好踩着低的桥面，比平日走路更瘸了。他勃然大怒说："这是世上最糟的一座桥。"

注 释

① 铁拐李：中国神话八仙之一，姓李，因瘸一腿，又使一根铁拐杖，故名。 One of the Eight Immortals in legend. His surname is Li. He is given the name because he had a lame leg and used an iron walking stick.

100. Iron Stick Li Crossing the Bridge

It is said the immortal Iron Stick Li once crossed a small bridge which was made by two planks, one thick and the other thin. So one side of the bridge was higher than the other side. The lame Iron Stick Li walked steadily, when crossing the bridge.

"This bridge is the best in the world," he said favourably.

But while returning, he crossed the bridge again from the opposite direction. This time Iron Stick Li's lame leg was on the low side and he became lamer than usual. "This is the worst bridge in the world," he said flying into a fury.

101. 蝙　蝠

凤凰生日，百鸟朝贺，唯独蝙蝠没有参加。过后，凤凰责问它：“你是我的下属，为何目中无人？”

蝙蝠回答：“我有腿，属于兽类，为什么要来给你拜寿？”

一天，麒麟过生日，众兽前往祝寿，蝙蝠也不去。麒麟批评了它。

蝙蝠说：“我有翅膀，属于禽类，为什么要来向你祝贺？”

有一次，麒麟遇到凤凰，谈起蝙蝠的事，互相慨叹说：“当今世态炎凉，偏偏又有这种不禽不兽之徒，谁对它也没有办法！”

101. The Bat

On the birthday of the phoenix, all the birds came to celebrate her birthday except for the bat. The phoenix reproached him, "You are my subordinate, why are you so supercilious?"

"I've legs, I belong to the animal classification. Why should I congratulate you on your birthday?"

One day when it was the unicorn's birthday, all kinds of animals came to celebrate with him, except for the bat. The unicorn criticized him.

"I've wings and belong to the bird classification, for what reason should I go to celebrate your birthday?" said the bat.

Once the unicorn met with the phoenix, they talked about the bat, and sighed with regret.

"Today the ways of the world suffer from inconstancy, and such a dispicable creature, neither bird nor animal," they said to each other, "and there's nothing that can be done about it."

102.贼 诗

从前闽①地有一个海贼叫郑广，后来投降朝廷，获得了官职。平日里，同僚们都瞧不起他。

在一次酒宴上，同僚们强要郑广赋诗一首，想当众让他出丑。但郑广不慌不忙，念了一首诗：

郑广有诗上众官，
彼此情况总一般。
诸位做官却做贼，
郑广做贼后当官。

郑广的诗明白如水，一语道破这群平日欺压、勒索钱财的贪官，其实与做贼没有什么不同。

注 释

① 闽：福建省的别称。 Another name of Fujian Province.

102. A Verse Composed By a Pirate

Once upon a time, in the Min area, there was a pirate named Zheng Guang. Later he surrendered to the imperial court and got an official position. But the other officials despised him.

At a dinner party his fellow officials forced Zheng to compose a poem in order to embarrass him. Zheng Guang calmly read out this verse:

For fellow officials Zheng Guang recites a poem,
How all have reached a category sinister,
First officials now lowly robbers on the roam,
While Zheng Guang, first a robber is now a minister.

His poem, clear as water, blurted out the truth, that greedy officials who extorted money and bullied people were no different from robbers.

责任编辑　叶　均
封面设计　李士伋

中国历代笑话精选(一)
程钦华　编注
*

华语教学出版社出版
中国北京百万庄路 24 号
邮政编码 100037
北京外文印刷厂印刷
中国国际图书贸易总公司发行
(中国北京车公庄西路 35 号)
北京邮政信箱第 399 号　邮政编码 100044
1991 年(40 开)第一版
1996 年第三次印刷
(汉英)
ISBN 7－80052－193－1/H・191(外)
01450
9－CE－2594PA